THE SIMPLE SECRETS
of HAPPINESS

THE SIMPLE SECRETS
of HAPPINESS

STORIES AND LESSONS
TO HELP YOU FIND
JOY IN LIFE
AND
FUFILLMENT IN WORK

Glenn Van Ekeren

Foreword by Jack Canfield and
Kimberly Kirberger

Prentice
Hall Press

CIP Data is available from the Library of Congress

Printed in the United States of America

Originally published as *12 Simple Secrets of Happiness* and *12 Simple Secrets of Happiness at Work*

10 9 8 7 6 5 4 3 2 1

ISBN 0-13-045202-5

PRENTICE HALL
Paramus, NJ 07652

http://www.phdirect.com

ACKNOWLEDGMENTS

My heartfelt thank you goes to the following people ...

To my wife, Marty, for her continual encouragement, friendship, and willingness to stick with me through thick and thin.

To my children, Matt and Katy, for believing in their dad and allowing me to tell stories about them.

To Lois Baartman and Jill Vanden Bosch, my fantastic assistants, who give of themselves without fanfare or recognition. I treasure our relationship.

To Phil Grove, my next door editor, who takes the time to read all of my writing with a sharp eye and always provides helpful insights to improve the message.

To my previous employer, Village Northwest Unlimited, who encouraged me to pursue my dreams.

CONTENTS

Contents

We have enjoyed tremendous success with the *Chicken Soup for the Soul*® books by sharing powerful stories of hope, inspiration, and encouragement with people of all ages—stories about people living their dreams, overcoming obstacles, and making a difference.

One of the people whose work we have drawn heavily on is Glenn Van Ekeren. We have used many stories from his previous books as well as his personal life in several of our Chicken Soup books.

That's why we are very excited and deeply honored to highly recommend Glenn's new book to you. We know you are going to love *The Simple Secrets of Happiness*. Glenn's unique storytelling ability combined with his commitment to people and his willingness to share his personal insights with his friends—which includes you, the reader—make this an extraordinary book. While you will find it inspiring and easy to read, you will also find that it is profound in its depth and, most important, easy to apply. When you apply these principles, you will see dramatic changes in your life.

As we are sure you are painfully aware, relationships these days can be a challenge. Whether it's a brother and sister relationship (like ours), a marriage, friendship, or a relationship with your co-workers, relationships take commitment, energy and a bit of Chicken Soup to warm the heart. Glenn offers loads of encouragement, solid support and lots of insightful understanding. Each selection goes right to the heart of real-world, timeless relationship principles.

Some pages will make you laugh. Others will get you thinking. Some will make you feel good. Others will encourage you to take action. And every page will fill you with a greater appreciation of yourself and how you can make a difference in the lives of others.

We have every confidence that with this book you are about to begin an enjoyable adventure, a journey that will lead you to more enriching and fulfilling relationships. The principles are all here. Read them! Believe them! Absorb them! But most important . . . apply them! The biggest secret in this book is this: If you work the principles, they will work for you!

Kimberly Kirberger
Jack Canfield

R elationships are as old as creation. They are the driving force behind most everything we do in life. The older I get, the more convinced I am of the direct correlation between our success with relationships and virtually everything of significance in life. When relationships are successful, life is good, but when they fail, along with them go health, prosperity, happiness and the joy of living.

Wherever we go. Whatever we do. No matter what career we have chosen or activity we are involved in, there is a common denominator . . . people. We can't live without them and sometimes it's tough to live with them. Relationships can be a source of wonderful fulfillment, satisfaction, and joy in life. They can also be a major pain in the neck. There is a constant pull between what we want our relationships to be and what they are. *The Simple Secrets of Happiness* is about those simple, yet often forgotten, accumulations of little things that contribute to building our relationships into what we want them to become.

So many books have been written about relationships; so many seminars given on the topic; and so many poems, songs and letters are inspired by them, that it might seem like the secrets to good relationships are known to everyone. Considering all the advice we've received, it should be easy to sustain harmonious, cooperative, and mutually beneficial relationships. In reality, we haven't reached that point. Maybe we read but don't respond, listen but don't understand, or know what to do but fail to take action. Whatever the case, relationships are either getting better, being nurtured, and growing, or they are slipping and sliding downhill.

The ability or inability to cultivate quality relationships is a choice. If we choose to live for ourselves, relationships will suffer and become dissonant. If we choose to focus our attention and invest our energies in our spouse, children, friends, neighbors, and co-workers we'll reap positive returns. Successful relationships are a natural outgrowth of the principle that the way we treat others affects the way they treat us. The tricky part is to not allow the way another person treats us to determine the way we treat that person.

I remember reading a *Dennis the Menace* cartoon where good old Mr. Wilson is sitting in his chair reading the newspaper. Mrs. Wilson is looking out the window as Dennis the Menace walks past the house. You can almost hear the sigh of relief from Mr. Wilson. He looks up from his paper and says to his wife, "There goes a Maalox moment waiting to happen."

It is virtually impossible to live through the day or week, much less a lifetime, without encountering someone who becomes our "Maalox moment." In the same breath, I must admit there are an equal number of people who radiate sunshine and encouragement wherever they go. They are the bright spots in our lives.

I can only hope that when people see me coming, or walking by, their first thought is not, "There goes the thorn in my life." I sincerely strive each day to be a positive influence in people's lives, to become what I often call a picker-upper person. These people are masters at building and maintaining quality relationships. They understand the dynamics for improving their casual and most intimate interaction. To them, love is a verb, and genuinely caring for others is a way of life. Picker-upper people transform lives and relationships by activating the qualities of a people builder.

This book is all about making a positive difference in people's lives. I probably wrote it for myself as much as anyone else. It contains the relationship principles I teach to audiences, preach to my children, and struggle to activate in my daily encounters. As I wrote, new ideas continually surfaced on ways in which I could improve my effectiveness with people. It is packed with timeless wisdom, proven principles, simple actions, and contemporary insight that will help you create increased enjoyment in your relationships.

You can become a picker-upper person. Choose any topic or any selection in this book and discover a variety of insightful comments, entertaining illustrations, and practical strategies that will help you:

Accept people for who they are.

Identify what people need to feel good about themselves.

Make your relationships bloom.

Get along with difficult people.

Effectively deal with conflict.

Develop a sincere interest in others.

Build on people's positive qualities.

Forgive hurtful actions.

Help others feel encouraged, uplifted and motivated to become all they can be.

Become the type of person people enjoy being around.

I assume that you're reading this book because you want more out of your relationships. If so, great! If you're looking for strategies to get your own way, sorry. If you want people to enjoy being with you, help is here. If you want a scheme to manipulate others, don't bother reading any further. If you're willing to commit yourself to the people in your life, the journey through the secrets of happiness shared with you in this book will be a pleasurable and beneficial one.

Renew your desire, increase your awareness and learn new skills to become a life-long picker-upper person. This down-to-earth and thought-provoking book is filled with insights for finding happiness through more fulfilling relationships. You'll be inspired to rekindle the warmth in your friendships, marriage, family, and work relationships.

THE SIMPLE SECRETS

of HAPPINESS

PART I

THE SIMPLE SECRETS *of* HAPPINESS IN LIFE

GENEROSITY

The measure of life is not its duration,
but its donation.

PETER MARSHALL

A GIVING
SPIRIT

Remember the biblical story of the widow's mite. Jesus watched the rich come to the temple to give their gifts for the temple treasury. He noticed a widow drop in two very small copper coins. Moved by her unselfish giving, Jesus told those who would hear that the value of her gift far exceeded all others. Most people gave gifts from their wealth. This poverty-stricken woman gave sacrificially.

It has been calculated that if the widow's two mites had been deposited in an account bearing 4-percent interest compounded semiannually, by today it would be valued at $4.8 billion trillion. Making a consistent small investment in people can also reproduce itself to create an outstanding return. A generous spirit exposes itself through an attitude that continually searches for ways to add value to people's lives. When a giving spirit permeates a relationship, the rewards are usually greater than either party expected. As Jesus commended the widow for her sacrificial giving, so, too, should we never underestimate the potential of the small things we do with the right motives.

In May of 1997, the Associated Press released a story about an outstanding high-school track runner and his sacrifice to help a teammate be successful. Troy Weiland ran for Canistota High School in South Dakota. He was an outstanding track star headed for Iowa State University on a track scholarship.

Troy decided his mission at the Danielsen Invitational track meet was to help his teammate Brad Jensen earn his varsity letter instead of scoring a victory for himself. If Jensen could finish sixth or better in the two-mile run, the varsity letter was his. Here's the play-by-play action as reported by the Associated Press.

"Troy kept telling me I was going to place," said Jensen. "Man, I was getting pumped."

For almost half the race, the runner trying to earn a varsity letter had one of the state's best high-school distance runners ever as his escort.

"Troy ran back with Jensen and kept an eye on the guys in the lead," said Canistota track coach Jerry Price. "I'd say he was about half a lap behind the leaders."

Weiland provided continual encouragement as he ran alongside Jensen.

"I said, 'Brad, you have to beat two people to place.' He was like 'OK, man, I can do this,'" Weiland said.

With a final few words of encouragement, Weiland took off for the leaders, now some 200 yards ahead, and not only caught them but soon lapped the field, coming upon Jensen again, who was battling another runner for seventh place, not good enough to place.

"Troy came up to me again and kept saying, 'You can do it,'" Jensen said. "He said if I kept running hard he was going to drop out. I said 'No, don't do that.' I tried to talk him out of it, but then he disappeared."

Weiland stepped off the track just before crossing the finish line. With Weiland out, Jensen now was battling for sixth place—good enough to earn his varsity letter.

Jensen used a late sprint to finish in sixth place. His time of 12:15 was 41 seconds faster than anything he had run before.

What a great story epitomizing a generous and giving spirit in a normally competitive environment. Not only is it difficult to get excited about other people's success but to

The miracle is this—the more we share, the more we have.

LEONARD
NIMOY

❀

give up your own success so someone else can be successful is virtually unheard of. Weiland's actions were captured by the press, recognized by teammates, and I guarantee you the fans were talking about his actions for days.

I'm not sure all happy people are generous, but I'm convinced that generous people are happy. Just remember you don't have to "be happy" to be generous, but your generosity will produce happiness—in others and you. John Bunyon believed, "You have not lived today until you have done something for someone who can never repay you." Give what little you can to someone who needs what you have and you'll not only produce happiness but the realization that life doesn't get much better than the internal rewards you'll experience.

A SCENARIO OF
TOUCHING KINDNESS

J erry Jenkins, writing for *Moody Monthly*, recalled a situation he observed while attending the premiere showing of Francis Schaeffer's film *How Should We Then Live?*. Dr. Schaeffer was fielding questions from the audience when a man with cerebral palsy struggled to ask a question. His slow, broken, and difficult-to-understand speech irritated some of the people in the audience. But not Schaeffer.

"I'm sorry," Schaeffer responded as the man finished his question. "Would you please repeat your last three words?" The man complied. "Now the last word one more time." The man again painstakingly repeated himself. Schaeffer went on to graciously answer the man's question.

Then, to the dismay of the audience, the young man had a second question. The entire process began again. Dr. Schaeffer continued to work kindly and patiently answering the question to the man's satisfaction.

People can do this for one another, can love one another with understanding.

HAROLD S.
KUSHNER

Keep in mind that the true meaning of an individual is how he treats a person who can do him absolutely no good.

ANN LANDERS

What would have been your reaction? Dr. Schaeffer revealed a kindness that set an example for the entire audience. He treated the man with a disability with the same dignity and respect he gave to others.

People don't care how much you know until you show them how much you care by your small acts of kindness. As you go about your daily activities, be especially giving to those who need your touch of kindness.

A SURPRISING ACT
OF COMPASSION

I read a great story about Fiorello H. LaGuardia. As New York City's mayor in 1935, he showed up in court one night in the poorest area of New York City and suggested the judge go home for the evening as he took over the bench.

LaGuardia's first case involved an elderly woman arrested for stealing bread. When asked whether she was innocent or guilty, this soft reply was offered, "I needed the bread, Your Honor, to feed my grandchildren." "I've no option but to punish you," the mayor responded. "Ten dollars or ten days in jail."

Proclaiming the sentence, he simultaneously threw $10 into his hat. He then fined every person in the courtroom 50 cents for living in a city "where a grandmother has to steal food to feed her grandchildren." Imagine the surprise of those in the room who I'm sure thought this was a black-and-white, open-and-shut case. When all had contributed their 50 cents, the woman paid her fine and left the courtroom with an additional $47.50.

How far you go in life depends on your being tender with the young, compassionate with the aged, sympathetic with the striving, and tolerant of the weak and strong, because someday in your life, you will have been all of these.

GEORGE
WASHINGTON
CARVER

Kindness in words creates confidence; kindness in thinking creates profoundness; kindness in giving creates love.

LAO-TSE

It has been said that kindness is the oil that takes the friction out of life. So often it is easy to be grit, rather than oil, by judging, condemning, or berating those going through trials and tribulations. Yet, an act or word of kindness can cool the friction and help someone keep pressing on. Look around you. To whom will you show generosity like that experienced by the grandmother?

SPEAK OF OTHERS
GRACIOUSLY

I don't think there is anything I despise worse than gossip. Gossips cause undue contention and strife. The wise King Solomon said, "The words of a whisperer are like dainty morsels, and they go down into the innermost parts of the body." Both the gossip and the unfortunate victim are injured by these "tiny morsels."

Listen to this conversation. Mary says, "Ellen told me you told her the secret that I asked you not to tell her." Alice responds, "Well, I told her I wouldn't tell you that she told me, so please don't tell her I did." Oh what a tangled web we weave when we betray someone's trust.

There will always be people who believe everything they hear and feel compelled to repeat it. Gossips are simply people with a "sense of rumor." Don't be one of them.

I remember occasions when word got back to me concerning a betrayed confidence. What a devastating feeling. Trust is destroyed and friendships are broken when the poisonous contents of a rumor leak.

There is so much good in the worst of us, and so much bad in the best of us, that it behooves all of us not to talk about the rest of us.

ROBERT LOUIS STEVENSON

Why do people gossip? Could it be that we think we make ourselves look better and gain greater acceptance with peers? Does confidential information make us feel important, more knowledgeable or superior so surely people will listen to us? Have you ever been jealous of somebody's achievements or the attention they receive, and by pointing out their weaknesses you look a little better? If somebody has injured us, how easy it is to put them in a bad light as a way of retaliating and balancing the scales. Gossip can also be used to win others to our side of a conflict. There is a tendency to think that the more people we can get to agree with us, the healthier our self-worth.

No matter what reason we give, there is no reason to gossip!

There is a legend about a person who went to the village priest for advice after repeating some slander about a friend and later finding out it wasn't true. He asked the priest what he could do to make amends for his thoughtless act.

The priest told the man: "If you want to make peace with yourself, you must fill a bag with feathers, and go to every door in the village, dropping a feather on each porch."

The peasant found a bag, filled it with feathers, and made his way throughout the village doing as he was told to do. He then returned to the priest and asked: "What else can I do?"

"There is one more thing," responded the priest, "take your bag and gather up every feather."

The peasant reluctantly began his quest to gather all the feathers he had distributed. Hours later he returned, saying, "I could not find all the feathers, for the wind had blown them away."

The priest responded, "So it is with gossip. Unkind words are easily dropped, but we can never take them back again."

The next time you are tempted to say an unkind, possibly untrue or unflattering word about someone, ask yourself how this information will benefit the receiver, yourself, and especially the person you are talking about. Be really clear on this one irrefutable fact: Once you say it, you can't take it back.

If you have an affinity for spreading rumors or welcoming gossip about other people, ask yourself if this is how you would want to be spoken of. Then strive to speak of others as you would want to be spoken of: only with graciousness and charity. And when you have nothing gracious or charitable to say, learn to say nothing at all.

A gossip is one who talks to you about others, a bore is one who talks to you about himself, and a brilliant conversationalist is one who talks to you about yourself.

LISA KIRK

HOPE

People love others not for who they are
but for how they make us feel.

IRWIN FEDERMAN

HOW DO YOU MAKE
PEOPLE FEEL?

I wish you could meet my daughter. Katy is a vibrant, enthusiastic young lady with a fabulous approach toward life. As a fourth grader, she committed herself to an enviable work ethic, developed a magnetic personality, and earned the respect of her teacher. (Of course, I'm entirely objective about my assessment.)

At the end of Katy's first semester as a fourth grader, a parent–teacher conference was scheduled for Thursday afternoon at 4:30 p.m. She was especially excitable during the week and confirmed the meeting time with her mother and me on several occasions. We assured her both of us planned to attend this special event.

On Wednesday morning Katy approached her teacher before school started. "I sure wish my conference was today!" she exclaimed. "Isn't tomorrow a good day for your parents to come?" her insightful teacher, Mrs. DeJong, queried.

"Oh no, they'll both be here," Katy responded, "I just wish my conference was today."

My son, here is the way to get people to like you. Make every person like himself a little better, and I promise that he or she will like you very much.

LORD CHESTERFIELD

❃

Fascinated by this unusual student attitude, Mrs. DeJong probed further. "Why would you like me to meet with your parents today, Katy?"

Katy flashed one of her heart-warming smiles as she blurted, "I just can't wait for them to come home and tell me how good I am!"

Being a good student, Katy knew the parent–teacher conference was one avenue for her to receive a bit of recognition. She also knew my wife and I made it a habit to discuss the conference with the kids. It doesn't take a rocket scientist to see why Katy was anxious for her conference. This was her opportunity to hear how good she was even though she already knew.

My wife and I have ample reason to support and encourage our children. They are good kids. I'm concerned that I spend far too little time looking for ways to encourage and an excessive amount of time searching for things to correct. It's amazing how conditioned I've become— conditioned to believe a parent's role is to correct, discipline, and direct. I'm all right with that when it's balanced with support, recognition, and encouragement. Oh, to find that perfect balance.

"Three billion people on the face of the earth go to bed hungry every night," said Cavett Robert. "But four billion people go to bed hungry for a simple word of encouragement and recognition."

Encouragers support our dreams, understand our difficulties, recognize our efforts, and celebrate our achievements with us. They keep us from going to bed with an aching stomach, broken heart, or damaged spirit. They seem to know what to say and when to say it. They provide nourishment for the soul. Encouragers build hope.

Become an encourager. Make it possible for people to say: "I like myself better when I'm with you."

THE SIMPLE SECRETS of HAPPINESS

LEARN TO GIVE
YOURSELF AWAY

Only those who
have learned the
power of sincere
and selfless
contribution
experience life's
deepest joy: true
fulfillment.

ANTHONY
ROBBINS

❁

There are two seas in the Holy Land. The famous Sea of Galilee takes in fresh water from a nearby brook, uses it to generate a variety of marine vegetation, and then passes it on to the Jordan River. The Jordan does its part by spreading the life throughout the desert, turning it into fertile land.

The Dead Sea, on the other hand, comes by its name for a reason—it's dead. The water in the Dead Sea is so full of salt that no life can exist. The major difference between these two bodies of water is that the Dead Sea takes in the water from the Jordan River and hangs on to it. It has no outlet.

What a perfect example of the differences in people. People who live without giving themselves away become stagnant and find that what they keep stifles their life. Those who freely give of themselves multiply life. Eric Butterworth said, "A committed giver is an incurable happy person, a secure person, a satisfied person, and a prosperous person."

There's a life-enhancing lesson here. If you don't sow anything today, you'll have nothing to reap in the future. A rich life is the direct result of enriching others. "Don't judge each day by the harvest you reap," advised Robert Louis Stevenson, "but by the seeds you plant."

According to a *New York Times* article, Mr. Milton Petrie enjoyed giving his money away. He researched New York papers "for stories of people life had kicked in the face. He then reached for his checkbook."

Petrie, the son of a Russian immigrant pawn-shop owner, built his fortune with a chain of women's clothing stores. When he died at the age of 92, his lifelong commitment to being a generous giver continued. The newspaper headline reporting his death said: MILLIONAIRE'S DEATH DOESN'T STOP HIS GENEROSITY. He reportedly named 451 beneficiaries of his $800 million estate.

"What keeps our interest in life and makes us look forward to tomorrow is giving pleasure to other people," advised Eleanor Roosevelt. "Happiness is not a goal, it is a by-product."

Did you know Elvis Presley never took a tax deduction for any of the millions of dollars he donated to charities? The "king" said he believed it would violate the spirit of giving.

General William Booth had a passion for the poor of London and committed himself to a mission of meeting those needs. By the time of his death, Booth's local mission had spread across the world. His final sermon, delivered from a hospital bed to an international convention of Salvation Army "soldiers," was simply a one-word telegram that read: "Others!"

Booth's one-word sermon encapsulated everything he believed about the purpose of living—giving unselfishly of yourself to benefit others.

Billionaire John D. Rockefeller lived the first part of his life as a miserable man, unable to sleep, feeling unloved, and surrounded by bodyguards. At age 53, he was diagnosed with a rare disease. He lost all of his hair, and his body became shrunken. Medical experts gave him a year to live.

Rockefeller started thinking beyond his current life and sought meaning to his existence. He gave away his money to churches and the poor, and he established the Rockefeller Foundation. His life turned around, his health improved, and contrary to the doctor's prediction, he lived to be 98.

John D. Rockefeller's life exemplified the transformation that's possible when the joy of giving is discovered. You might be tempted to think that if you had Rockefeller's wealth, giving to others would be easy. Although it's easy to find examples of people with wealth who gave it away, what we're talking about here is much more than writing a check to your favorite charity. That's only a minute portion of the message.

"Every person passing through life will unknowingly leave something and take something away," reflected Robert Fulghum. "Most of this 'something' cannot be seen or heard or numbered. It does not show up in a census. But nothing counts without it."

Dwight Moody made this "something" Fulghum alluded to a way of life. Moody said, "I wish to do all the good I can, for all the people I can, in as many ways as I can, for as long as I can."

You can keep the waters of life flowing and add tremendous value to others by giving yourself to others. Put others first in your thinking. Find ways to enrich their lives. Give unselfishly. It is a natural law of life that the more of

Lock your house, go across the railroad tracks, find someone in need, and do something for him.

DR. KARL
MENNINGER

❧

yourself you pass on to others with no expectation of receiving in return, the more your life will be blessed.

If you want to experience ongoing success, learn to give yourself away and give hope to others. "Success is not rare—it is common," believed Henry Ford, Sr. "It is a matter of adjusting one's efforts to obstacles and one's abilities to a service needed by others. There is no other possible success. But most people think of it in terms of getting; success, however, begins in terms of giving."

YOU CAN MAKE
A DIFFERENCE

L et's suppose for a moment you just received a card in the mail from your best friend. The message it contained went like this:

First, I want to apologize. I've intended to send you this card for several months but never got around to it.

You are a special person! I appreciate your acceptance of me just the way I am, and your friendship is the most valuable thing I have. I marvel at your positive attitude toward work, family, and life in general. It shows in everything you do. Thank you for being an exemplary role model. Most of all, I appreciate you for being you.

Have a great day!

How would you feel? Would you sense a tinge of embarrassment along with a broad internal smile? How might

The purpose of life is not to win. The purpose of life is to grow and to share. When you come to look back on all that you have done in life, you will get more satisfaction from the pleasure you have brought into other people's lives than you will from the time that you outdid and defeated them.

RABBI HAROLD KUSHNER

21

this note affect your day, your interactions at work, or your feelings about yourself? Most important, how many times have you sent or received such an encouraging message?

Contrast that uplifting scenario with the reality of how many people feel about their relationships. The following story from John Powell, S.J.'s *Will the Real Me Please Stand Up?* sadly but realistically depicts the dire need for us to become sensitive to the needs of those around us.

"Early on Sunday morning, August 5, 1962, Marilyn Monroe was found dead. The coroner would later call it 'suicide.' When Marilyn's maid discovered her lifeless body on that Sunday morning, she noticed that the phone by her bedside was dangling off the hook. Marilyn had obviously made a last attempt to communicate with someone. When her last attempt failed, she gave up and died alone.

"Claire Booth Luce wrote a poignant article for Life magazine entitled, 'What Really Killed Marilyn?: The Love Goddess who never found any love.' Luce suggests that the dangling phone was an apt symbol of Marilyn's life. She tried for a long time to say that she was a person, but few ever took her seriously. Only after her death on a Saturday night, when all beautiful women are assumed to be out on the arm of a handsome escort, did many of the facts of her life surface.

"Marilyn Monroe was seriously disliked by most of her Hollywood contemporaries. She was dubbed a 'prima donna.' Very often, she would arrive hours late for a filming. As she casually strolled into the studio, no one suspected that she had been at her home nervously vomiting. She was terrified, afraid of cameras. No doubt her emotional reactions were the result of a sad and troubled childhood. Her father, an itinerant banker, had deserted the family. Her mother was repeatedly committed to mental institutions. Marilyn was raped at age eight by a boarder in her foster home. She was given a nickel not to tell.

"Now at age 35, her mirror kept telling her that the only thing others ever noticed about or praised in her was fading. She must have felt like an artist who is losing his vision or a musician whose hands are becoming arthritic. Marilyn had endured a painful childhood, had moved through several marriages, and had made many movies, but few ever took her seriously . . . until she was dead."

We need each other, yet we live in an age where actions of kindness and encouragement are far too rare. There is a tendency to be nit-picking and fault-finding and often positive, uplifting messages are buried in the desire to make people what we want them to be rather than appreciating them for who they are. We must learn to appreciate and find joy in our relationships, rather than constantly seek to reform those with whom we interact. We must learn to spread hope when others only express despair.

The chance to make a difference in someone's life can present itself at home, at work, with friends or strangers.

Look for an opportunity to lift someone's spirits, to make someone feel appreciated. Opportunities for offering hope to others present themselves everyday, we just have to pay attention and tune in.

As Albert Einstein stated, "Man is here for the sake of other men—above all for those upon whose smile and well-being our own happiness depends, and also for the countless unknown souls, with whose fate we are connected by a bond of sympathy."

KINDNESS

*Our worst fault is our preoccupation with
the faults of others.*

KAHLIL GIBRAN

BEWARE OF BECOMING
A FAULT-FINDER

C harlie Brown suffered from the "can't-do-anything-right" syndrome. Lucy is always there to remind him of the error of his ways.

On one occasion Lucy puts her hands on her hips and says, "You, Charlie Brown, are a foul ball in the line drive of life! You're in the shadow of your own goal posts! You are a miscue! You are three putts on the eighteenth green! You are a seven–ten split in the tenth frame! You are a dropped rod and reel in the lake of life! You are a missed free throw, a shanked nine iron, and a called third strike! Do you understand? Have I made myself clear?"

As unfair as Kahlil Gibran's comment might seem, that "Our worst fault is our preoccupation with the faults of others," the tendency to be a Lucy is tempting. How easy it is to point out to people what they aren't, haven't been, or never will become. Whether you are raising a family, running a company, or building a relationship, be sensitive to these words of wisdom from Will Rogers: "There is nothing as easy as denouncing. It don't take much to see that something is wrong, but it does take some eyesight to see what will put it right again."

In most cases, criticism is a futile and destructive process. It forces people to be defensive and usually causes them to make attempts at justifying their actions. Insensitivity will bruise pride, reduce people's sense of importance, and promote resentment within our relationships.

Have you thought lately about someone you would like to change, control, or improve? Fine. Begin with yourself. It has been said that most of us find it difficult to accept the imperfections in others that we possess ourselves. It's uncomfortable to watch people displaying the same negative qualities we ourselves have been unable to overcome. Confucius once said: "Don't complain about the snow on your neighbor's roof when your own doorstep is unclean." Attempting first to improve ourselves will provide us with a greater degree of tolerance concerning the weaknesses or undesirable traits of others.

The late John Wanamaker once reflected, "I learned 30 years ago that it is foolish to scold. I have enough trouble overcoming my own limitations without fretting over the fact that God has not seen fit to distribute evenly the gift of intelligence." Using Wanamaker's advice, concentrate on "me" first, with my heavy load of shortcomings, faults, and areas needing improvement. This enhances my ability to accept the limitations of others.

If you're thinking, "I wish my spouse, boss, friend would read this," then the message hasn't soaked in. Avoiding a fault-finding lifestyle is first and foremost your responsibility. An upbeat, encouraging, nourishing relationship begins with you.

Most fault-finding begins with something like this: "Perhaps I shouldn't say this, but . . ." Another common way to slip into critical remarks is by prefacing our comments with, "I don't mean to criticize, but . . ." And then we go on to do what? Criticize. Once we've shared our inspired observations, we justify them by saying: "I was only trying to help."

There is a huge gap between destructive criticism and constructive feedback that grows out of a sincere desire to enrich someone's life. You can make a positive difference in someone's life by avoiding a fault-finding approach and endorsing a spirit of affirmation and help. Consider these approaches:

1. Uphold People's Self Esteem. "I give up." "What's the use?" "I never do anything right." These are common feelings of people who feel defeated and deflated by personal attacks.

The apostle Paul wrote to the church in Rome: "Why then do you criticize your brother's actions, why do you try to make him look small?" Looking small hurts. People can tell us all day long how wonderful we are and how great it is to be our friend. Then one person criticizes us and we are devastated. The human recorder plays that tape over and over, forgetting the positives and bemoaning the one critical comment.

Be kind. Be gentle. Never forget that a person's spirit is easily crushed. Let people know how much you care for them before ever offering corrective advice. After giving negative feedback, offer additional affirmation of your respect, love, and concern for the person.

2. Focus on Abilities Rather than on Vulnerabilities. I've never met a person who has the ability to do anything worthwhile using his or her weaknesses. Tell people what you like about their performance before you suggest improvement. Find something, no matter how small or insignificant it might seem, that you can compliment them for. It's much easier to swallow criticism that is preceded by a sincere affirmation of what we do well.

3. Check Your Motives. Criticism is often an attempt to raise our own self-concept by comparing our faults to the weaknesses we observe in others. If I can point out some glitch in your life, then mine doesn't look so bad. When I am especially sensitive to an area in my life that needs adjustment, it is wise for me to be careful about what I am looking for in others. Lord Chesterfield said, "People hate those who make them feel their own inferiority." Ouch! Are you really trying to help or are you motivated by an effort to boost your own ego? An unknown author adds, "It is often our own imperfection which makes us reprove the imperfection of others; a sharp-sighted self-love of our own which cannot pardon the self-love of others."

Alice Duer Miller advised: "If it's painful for you to criticize your friends—you're safe in doing it. But if you take the slightest pleasure in it—that's the time to hold your tongue."

4. Keep Your Attitude in Check. Fault-finding communicates the attitude: "I want you to feel as miserable as

A critic is someone who never actually goes to the battle yet who afterwards comes out shooting the wounded.

TYNE DALY

❀

I do." We don't actually say that to others. Think about it. When do you criticize others the most? When life is flowing along like a dream? Probably not. How about when you are experiencing a trying day? Being sensitive to your emotions will help you refrain from communicating an attitude that because you're a crab, someone is about to get dumped on. Be careful not to blame others for the way you feel.

5. Offer Assistance. "What can I do to help?" That is a powerful question. Abraham Lincoln believed that, "He has a right to criticize who has a heart to help."

Fault-finding poisons people's spirits. It chips away at self-worth. Withdrawal seeks security. Defensiveness surfaces. Trust is broken. Love wilts. Growth, cooperation, love, sensitivity, encouragement, and understanding cannot exist in a relationship plagued with criticism. If you persist in pointing out limitations, destruction is imminent.

Offer caring suggestions. Discuss unmet expectations honestly and objectively. Provide educated advice. Encourage people to be the best they can be. Accept people for who they are—mistakes and all.

ENLARGE YOUR CIRCLE
OF INFLUENCE

H ow thick is your Rolodex? How many people have you determined important enough to list in the telephone and address section of your day planner? When is the last time you added someone to your list of valued resources?

How many times have you entered the room of a meeting, seminar, social gathering, or community event and quickly scanned the audience to find someone you know? How many interesting people did you overlook by cozying up to and attaching yourself to familiar people?

Not only is it advisable to align yourself with activities and a lifestyle that breeds a broader vision of life, but it is equally important to align yourself with an ever expanding circle of influence. Surround yourself with exceptional people who have discovered the world in a way different from you.

Most of us become so comfortable with our acquaintances. We play golf with the same foursome, associate with the

I am going to be meeting people today who talk too much— people who are selfish, egotistical, ungrateful. But I wouldn't be surprised or disturbed, for I can't imagine a world without such people.

MARCUS AURELIUS

same people at work, have lunch with our select network, attend social events with a small inner circle, and enjoy philosophical conversation with those we have repeated the same conversation with over and over.

Capitalize on and create every window of opportunity possible to get acquainted with at least one new person every week. Step out of your comfort zone and introduce yourself to someone.

When you fill up with gas next time, strike up a conversation with the gas station attendant. Ask your next server at the restaurant about the most interesting situation he or she dealt with that day. When ordering over the phone from mail-order catalogs, question the order takers about the things they enjoy most about their job. Make contact with a half dozen people in your community and ask them to tell you about their profession.

The opportunities are endless. But, you must begin seeing every person you encounter as an opportunity to learn, grow, and expand your intelligence.

Blast through the barriers of shyness, fear, self-consciousness, or even apathy to show others how interested you are in their lives and experiences. You'll be amazed how accommodating people are when you express a sincere interest in them. It takes a variety of people to challenge us, encourage us, promote us, and most of all, help us achieve a broader dimension of ourselves.

DON'T OVERLOOK LITTLE ACTS
OF KINDNESS

At the hour of death, when we come face to face with God, we are going to be judged on love—not how much we have done, but how much love we put into our actions.

MOTHER TERESA

❀

Calvin Coolidge was invited to a dinner hosted by Dwight Morrow, the father of Anne Morrow Lindbergh. After Coolidge had excused himself for the evening, Morrow expressed his belief that Coolidge would make a good president. The others disagreed and a discussion ensued concerning Coolidge's qualifications. Those not believing in his presidential potential felt he was too quiet and lacked charisma and personality. He just wasn't likable enough, they said.

Anne, then age six, spoke up. "I like him," she said. Displaying a finger with a bandage around it, she continued, "He was the only one at the party who asked about my sore finger, and that's why he would make a good president," said little Anne.

Anne had a good point. Maybe asking a little girl about her sore finger isn't necessarily a bona fide qualification for the presidency, but a spirit of kindness is a surefire way to impress others. Kindness, the sincere expression of love, makes the people around you feel loved and valuable.

Opportunities to show kindness abound. If someone were to pay you 10 cents for every kindness you ever showed and would collect 5 cents for every unkind word or action, would you be rich or poor?

Flash a smile to those you meet on the street. William Arthur Ward believed, "A warm smile is the universal language of kindness."

Use the precious words "please" and "thank you" at every possible occasion. St. Ambrose suggested that "no duty is more urgent than that of returning thanks."

Show concern for those inflicted with little hurts and big ones. Allow others to go in front of you in the grocery line (that's a tough one for me). Make it possible for people to change lanes in heavy traffic. Open the door for someone entering the same building as you. Offer a warm greeting to people you meet walking in hotel hallways.

You might be saying, "Isn't this a bit simplistic?" You're right. But, remember what impressed Anne Morrow? It was a sensitive expression of concern for a bandaged finger that made a positive impression. Simple? Maybe. Effective?

When we remember our unkindness to friends who have passed beyond the veil, we wish we could have them back again, if only for a moment, so that we could go on our knees to them and say, "Have pity and forgive."

MARK TWAIN

No doubt. It's the consistency of our little acts of kindness that cause people to smell a pleasant aroma about us wherever we go.

"Spread your love everywhere you go," encouraged Mother Teresa. "First of all in your own house. Give love to your children, to your wife or husband, to a next-door neighbor . . . let no one ever come to you without leaving better and happier. Be the living expression of God's kindness; kindness in your face, kindness in your eyes, kindness in your smile, kindness in your warm greeting."

RANDOM ACTS OF KINDNESS

I read a story about a woman who answered the knock on her door to find a man with a sad expression.

"I'm sorry to disturb you," he said, "but I'm collecting money for an unfortunate family in the neighborhood. The husband is out of work, the kids are hungry, the shelves are bare, the utilities will soon be cut off, and worse, they're going to be kicked out of their apartment if they don't pay the rent by this afternoon."

"I'd be happy to help out," said the woman with great concern. "But who are you?"

"I'm the landlord," he replied.

Suffice it to say the landlord is not an enviable example of kindness. At the same time we can probably all relate to times when kindness was used to get our own way or to convince someone to do something that would benefit us. But pure kindness flows from pure motives.

According to the Associated Press, Chuck Wall, a human-relations instructor at Bakersfield College in California, was watching a local news program one day when a cliché from a

Never lose sight of the fact that the most important yardstick of your success will be how you treat other people—your family, friends, and co-workers, and even strangers you meet along the way.

BARBARA BUSH

broadcaster caught his attention: "Another random act of senseless violence."

Wall got an idea. He gave an unusual and challenging assignment to his students. They were to do something out of the ordinary to help someone and then write an essay about it.

One thing led to another. Wall then dreamed up a bumper sticker that read, "Today, I will commit one random act of senseless KINDNESS . . . Will You?" Students sold the bumper stickers for one dollar each and donated the profits to a county Braille center.

An impressive variety of acts of kindness were performed. One student paid his mother's utility bills. Another student bought 30 blankets from the Salvation Army and took them to homeless people gathered under a bridge.

The idea expanded. Bumper stickers were slapped on all 113 county patrol cars. The message was trumpeted from the pulpits, in schools, and was endorsed by professional associations.

As Chuck Wall reflected on the success of his idea, he commented, "I had no idea our community was in such need of something positive."

It's not just Mr. Wall's community that needs random acts of kindness.

After Wausau, Wisconsin was featured as the subject of a negative story on *60 Minutes*, *The Wausau Daily Herald* talked area businesses into co-sponsoring a Random Acts of Kindness Week.

Businesses, organizations, and individuals were encouraged to perform simple acts of kindness for people they knew or didn't know. The response was astronomical. Over 200 businesses and organizations participated. The employees of the newspaper went out wearing T-shirts bearing the Random Acts of Kindness slogan, and they performed good deeds.

Banks washed car windows in the drive-up lanes, church groups mowed lawns for people in the neighborhood, movie theaters gave out free passes to people waiting in line. One individual walked into a restaurant and bought a cup of coffee for every person in the place. The newspaper ran a hot line for people to phone in the acts of kindness they had witnessed. More than 500 calls were received. The response was so tremendous that *The Wausau Daily Herald* decided to repeat the event the next year.

How about creating a random-acts-of-kindness lifestyle. Your motto could be, "Everyday in some way I will show kindness to someone who is not in a position to repay me." You might be amazed at how the idea grows.

Courtesy is the one coin you can never have too much of or be stingy with.

JOHN WANAMAKER

FRIENDSHIP

*A friend is someone we can count on for
understanding, support, discretions,
and, if we're lucky, insight, wisdom,
and well-timed foolishness.*

JOHN R. O'NEIL

PORTRAIT
OF A FRIENDSHIP

O ut of the *Book of Sunshine* came this portrait of a friendship:

Those who turn their radio dials to sports commentaries will perhaps have relished this human interest story of President Dwight Eisenhower.

It occurred in a little town in Kansas, where Dwight Eisenhower spent his boyhood days. He was a comely lad, strong and virile, filled with the spirit of an athlete. He chose boxing as his pastime, and his ambition and skilled technique soon made him the champion boxer of the town. There was none who dared challenge young Eisenhower's prowess.

But one day, there came to town another young man. He gave his name as Frankie Brown. Brown bore the reputation of a professional boxer, and he soon learned of the ambitious young Eisenhower. A match was arranged between the two young athletes. No one was ever able to tell who won the honors, but both fought so well that before the bout was over, the two were fast friends.

The easiest kind of relationship for me is with ten thousand people. The hardest is with one.

JOAN BAEZ

They retired to a restaurant following the affair, and there they discussed plans for their future. Eisenhower desired to go to college, but Brown wanted to pursue boxing as a professional career. Eisenhower sought to persuade Brown first to acquire the higher schooling. In the wee hours of the night, the two emerged, both determined to go to college.

Frankie Brown entered Notre Dame. The determination that led him to follow Dwight Eisenhower's advice also stood him in hand in becoming the noted and beloved football coach of Notre Dame—Knute Kenneth Rockne.

In a fateful hour on March 31, 1931, the airplane in which Knute Rockne was enroute to his old friend in Kansas crashed to earth, crushing a life that had matched the determination and friendship and prowess of an Eisenhower.

Once, while sitting in a restaurant, Henry Ford, Sr. was asked: "Who is your best friend?"

Ford thought for a moment, then took out his pencil and wrote in large letters on the tablecloth: "He is your best friend who brings out of you the best that is in you."

Rockne and Eisenhower's friendship exemplified this belief. They challenged each other, encouraged each other to raise the bar on their personal expectations, and built a relationship around mutual respect. That combination inspired Knute Rockne and Dwight Eisenhower to reach for their potential.

It's enjoyable having friends who make us laugh. I cherish those friends who offer sincere advice. Friends who want to understand what's important to me are so valuable. I deeply respect those friends who genuinely celebrate my successes and encourage me through the failures. I don't want to leave out those friends who help me maintain my childlike, fun spirit. But the friend who challenges me to be all God intended me to be can't be replaced. Everybody needs a friend like that.

ARE YOU FILLING PEOPLE UP OR SUCKING THEM DRY?

To do something, however small, to make others happier and better is the highest ambition, the most elevating hope, which can inspire a human being.

JOHN
LUBBOCK

❀

I'm more convinced than ever before that success and fulfillment in life are in direct proportion to the investment we make in people. If someone spent the whole day with you, how would they feel at the end of the day—filled up or sucked dry? Are you the kind of person who searches for ways to inject hope, encouragement, and goodwill, or do you tend to extract those necessities in your daily interaction?

The good news is that no one needs to live a minute longer extracting life out of people. We can all increase our building, filling, and replenishing habits and thereby make it possible for people to like themselves and their lives better when they're with us. Consider a few practical actions to put on your daily relationship agenda.

1. Remember the Basics. In 1860, the *Lady Elgin* collided with a lumber barge on a stormy night and sank, leaving 393 people stranded in the waters of Lake Michigan. Two hundred seventy-nine of these people drowned. A young college student named Edward Spencer plunged into the water again and again to rescue people. After he had pulled 17 people from the freezing water, he was overcome with exhaustion and collapsed, never to stand again. For the remainder of his life, Spencer was confined to a wheelchair. Years later, someone asked him his most vivid memory of that fateful night. "The fact that not one of the 17 ever returned to thank me," was his reply, according to a Chicago newspaper.

I'm sure you would agree that this is unthinkable. How could 17 people, who had their lives spared because of this young man, fail to show their gratitude? Before we judge them too harshly, it might be worth our time to evaluate our consistency in remembering life's basic manners. Smile. Say "please" and "thank you." Use people's first names when speaking with them. Greet people with a hearty "hello!" or "good morning!" Show interest in your coworkers' welfare. Maintain a positive, optimistic outlook on matters other people tend to scowl at. Think about how others feel. Be an advocate of dignity and respect for all people.

The value of these basics is often overlooked, taken for granted, or missed completely. These simple actions communicate the caring and compassionate attitude encouragers possess. Review the list and find ways to continually do the little acts of kindness that produce big dividends.

2. Honk an Encouraging Message. Have you ever noticed how some friendships, marriages, and parent–child relationships are vibrant and growing while others seem to be plagued with discouragement? It may be a difference in attitude. If people build up and encourage one another, the whole atmosphere is refreshing. But a critical, negative spirit breeds tension and conflict.

Bruce Larson, in his book *Wind and Fire*, illustrates the power of encouragement. Writing about sandhill cranes, he said, "These large birds who fly great distances across continents have three remarkable qualities. First, they rotate leadership. No one bird stays out in front all the time. Second, they choose leaders who can handle turbulence. And then (this is my favorite), all during the time one bird is leading, the rest are honking affirmation."

Conduct an attitude check. Are you critical of people, situations, and life in general? Do you complain about the job someone else is doing or should have done? Do you have a negative spirit? If so, work to become a positive honking friend, spouse, parent, and coworker. Negative sourpusses are energy suckers. Positive horn honkers inspire others to fly further and higher.

Isn't it amazing how applicable the unique habits of a sandhill crane are to us. When people consistently build up and encourage, the whole atmosphere of their relationship is nurturing. People feel safe, comfortable taking risks, and they experience healthier feelings about themselves. Virginia Arcastle said, "When people are made to feel secure, important, and appreciated, it will no longer be necessary for them to whittle down others in order to seem bigger in comparison."

Check your interactions. What kind of messages have you been honking lately?

3. Believe in People. Dale Carnegie said, "Tell a child, a husband, or an employee that he is stupid or dumb at a certain thing, that he has no gift for it, and that he is doing it all wrong and you have destroyed almost every incentive to try to improve. But use the opposite technique; be liberal with encouragement; make the thing seem easy to do; let the other person know that you have faith in his ability to do it, that he has an undeveloped flair for it—and he will practice until the dawn comes in at the window in order to excel."

According to a selection in the March 1992 *Homemade*, a young man in London wanted to be a writer, but the cards seemed stacked against him. He had only four years of school, and his father was in jail because he couldn't pay his debts. Just to survive the pain of hunger, the young man got a job pasting labels on bottles in a rat-infested warehouse. He slept in an attic with two other boys from the slums. With such little confidence in himself and in his ability to write, he secretly slipped out in the middle of the night to mail his first manuscript so nobody would laugh at his dream. That manuscript, along with countless others, was rejected. Finally, one story was accepted. He wasn't paid anything, but the editor praised him for his writing. That one little compliment caused him to wander aimlessly through the streets with tears rolling down his cheeks. The compliment inspired him to continue and improve. It also led to a brilliant career for Charles Dickens.

Donald Laird said, "Always help people increase their own self-esteem. Develop your skill in making other people feel important. There is hardly a higher compliment you can pay an individual than helping him be useful and to find satisfaction from his usefulness."

Expressing our belief and faith in people can provide the inspiration for people to pursue their dreams. Find the seed of achievement waiting for your nourishment. Help people believe in themselves more than they believe in themselves and watch them blossom.

4. Express Your Love. I fear too many of us might be represented by the guy who exclaimed to his wife, "Honey, when I think about how much I love you, I can hardly keep from telling you."

Telling someone how much they mean to you seems like a basic relationship action. And it should be. But it's not. We may want to tell others how much they mean to us, but we don't. We want to hear words of love and affection and are disappointed at how infrequent those messages touch our ears. By our very nature, our hearts respond to a message of love.

In his book *In the Arena*, former President Richard Nixon reflected on the depression he experienced following his resignation from the presidency and then undergoing surgery. At the depths of his discouragement, he told his wife, Pat, that he just wanted to die.

At Mr. Nixon's lowest point, a nurse entered the room, pulled open the drapes, and pointed to a small airplane flying back and forth. The plane was pulling a banner that read: GOD LOVES YOU AND SO DO WE. This powerful, uplifting expression of love was arranged by Ruth Graham, evangelist Billy Graham's wife. Nixon said this was a turning point. Realizing someone cared lifted his spirits and gave him the courage and desire to press on.

Somebody once said, "Appreciating others without telling them is like winking at someone in the dark. You know what you're doing, but nobody else does."

Don't just think about expressing your love and appreciation for those you care about. Take the initiative. Don't wait for the other person—the two of you could wait a long time. Never assume people know how you feel about them. Give someone close to you a hug, pat him on the back and say, "I love you," or "You mean a lot to me," or "I care about you."

It feels good.

Someone might say, "I'm not into this 'touchy-feely' stuff. I'm uncomfortable giving hugs or verbal praise." If you're saying "amen" to that, here's another option. Write a letter or send a note to brighten someone's day. Who could benefit from a note of appreciation, word of concern, or a card complimenting her for a job well done? Don't let the impulse slip by without taking action. Tread yourself a well-worn path to the mailbox.

5. Uphold People's Self-Esteem. I like Henry Ward Beecher's observation that "There are persons so radiant, so genial, so kind, so pleasure-bearing, that you instinctively feel good in their presence that they do you good, whose coming into a room is like bringing a lamp there."

I had the privilege of working several years as a volunteer with junior-high-age youth in a basketball program. It would be self-gratifying to say I was always the type of person Beecher described, but I wasn't. I did learn, however, that when I built young people's self-esteem, they were open to instruction.

Imagine 12-year-old Laurie struggling to get the little round ball through the round cylinder. She's zero for ten and you approach her saying, "Laurie, I like the way you put everything into your shot. I think you're going to make a good basketball player."

Laurie beams. She is receptive and eager to learn more. Laurie is all ears when you add, "Laurie, you tend to throw your elbow out and shoot off your palms. Let me show you the proper shooting method."

Sounds simple, doesn't it. The beauty is, upholding a person's self-esteem is simple, if our motives are right. Rather than being intent on correction, let your instruction be grounded in affirmation.

The following illustration from *Our Daily Bread* puts the finishing touches on the importance of upholding self-esteem. Benjamin West was just trying to be a good baby-sitter for his little sister, Sally. While his mother was out, Benjamin found some bottles of colored ink and proceeded to paint Sally's portrait. But by the time Mrs. West returned, ink blots stained the table, chairs, and floor. Benjamin's mother surveyed the mess without a word until she saw the picture. Picking it up she exclaimed, "Why, it's Sally!" And she bent down and kissed her young son.

In 1763, when he was 25 years old, Benjamin West was selected as history painter to England's King George III. He became one of the most celebrated artists of his day. Commenting on his start as an artist, he said, "My mother's kiss made me a painter."

Each of us yearns for someone to fill us, build us, and lift us up. We encounter plenty of people along the way intent on letting us know where we've failed, fallen short of expectations, or about what areas of our life are less than perfect. These energy suckers are a dime a dozen. We need people who make us feel valued and worthwhile just as we are.

Make it possible for people to say, "I like myself better when I'm with you."

Remember the basics, honk encouraging words, believe in people more than they believe in themselves, freely express your love, and uphold people's self-esteem.

Do not do unto others as you think they should do unto you. Their tastes may not be the same.
GEORGE
BERNARD SHAW

A GIVING
SPIRIT

*To keep the fire
burning
brightly, keep
the two logs
together, near
enough to keep
each other
warm, and far
enough
apart—about
a finger's
breadth—for
breathing
room. Good
fire, good
marriage—
same rule.*

MARNIE REED
CROWELL

Some married couples insist every moment of their lives be occupied with each other.

Relationship experts indicate that healthy marriages are interdependent, where couples are comfortable in situations requiring independence and where they even enjoy periodic dependency. Just as with any friendship, danger occurs when neither person has learned to be independent. Obsessive dependency can destroy relationships but can also inhibit the opportunity to learn self-sufficiency.

An article in the February 3, 1984 *Los Angeles Times* told of a couple in Vista, California, who took ill at the same time. The article tells how Harry and Cora Walker were inseparable in their 50 years of living together. When they took ill they went to the hospital and Harry was admitted into one room with pneumonia while Cora was admitted to another room with a kidney ailment. They visited each other daily, but within a few days Harry took a turn for the worse and died. Eight hours after her husband's passing, Cora was dead, too.

Marital interdependence is an outgrowth of a person's healthy independence. When we learn to seek the best within ourselves and our partner, there is joy in living whether together or apart.

A marriage is like a long trip in a tiny rowboat: If one passenger starts to rock the boat, the other has to steady it; otherwise, they will go to the bottom together.

DAVID
REUBEN

EMPATHY

We're all in this together—by ourselves.

LILY TOMLIN

A CURE FOR THE LONELY

The unfortunate truth in Lily Tomlin's comment came to life in October of 1993 when the major television networks covered a story from Worcester, Massachusetts. Police found a woman dead on her kitchen floor. Adele Gaboury died of natural causes at age 73—four years before she was found. No one missed her.

How can this be? How can any human being go unmissed for four years? According to the Associated Press, neighbors had notified authorities years earlier when they noticed an unusual amount of accumulated mail and newspapers and that the lawn was virtually unkempt.

When the police notified Ms. Gaboury's brother, he indicated she had gone into a nursing home. Police notified the postal service to stop delivering mail. Neighbors stepped in to care for the yard and have the utility company shut off the water when a pipe froze, broke, and sent water flowing out under the door. No one suspected Ms. Gaboury's lifeless body was stretched out inside.

Warmth, kindness, and friendship are the most yearned for commodities in the world. The person who can provide them will never be lonely."

ANN LANDERS

Loneliness is the prison of the human spirit.

JOHN POWELL, S.J.

❋

One friend from the past commented, "She didn't want anyone bothering her at all. I guess she got her wish, but it's awfully sad."

According to newspaper reports, Adele lived in her house in this middle-class neighborhood for 40 years, but none of her neighbors knew her well. "My heart bleeds for her," a neighbor was quoted as saying, "but you can't blame a soul. If she saw you out there, she never said hello to you."

I have to believe Adele Gaboury lived in a lonely world. She was surrounded by people, yet alone. Although it appears she made little effort to reach out to those around her, it's evident few people showered her with attention.

This unfortunate scenario reminds us that giving and receiving are interdependent. They work together to form the natural laws that govern our relationships. What we give to others, we'll get. What we send out, comes back to us. What we sow, we reap. In other words, what goes around comes around. Simply put, when you reach out to meet the needs of other people, your needs will be met.

We can learn a valuable lesson from Adele Gaboury's experience. What if Adele and her neighbors had understood and lived out the natural laws? Smiled. Been friendly. Offered assistance. Performed kind deeds. Been generous. Been nice. Showed courtesy. Shared love. A multitude of other gestures would have produced a like response.

But we must be willing to share these expressions to receive them. A lonely life and unnoticed death are unnecessary. Be patient and persistent in seeking out opportunities to unselfishly give of yourself to meet the needs of others. Don't hesitate. "You cannot do a kindness too soon," said Ralph Waldo Emerson, "for you never know how soon it will be too late."

The most terrible poverty is loneliness and the feeling of being unwanted.

MOTHER TERESA

MAKE A DIFFERENCE
IN PEOPLE'S LIVES

Doing nothing for others is the undoing of one's self. We must be purposely kind and generous or we miss the best part of existence. The heart that goes out of itself gets large and full of joy. This is the great secret of the inner life. We do ourselves the most good by doing something for others.

HORACE MANN

A wise and beloved shah once ruled the land of Persia. He cared deeply for his people and wanted only what was best for them. The Persians knew this shah took a personal interest in their affairs and tried to understand how his decisions affected their lives. Periodically he would disguise himself and wander through the streets, trying to see life from their perspective.

One day he disguised himself as a poor village man and went to visit the public baths. Many people were there enjoying the fellowship and relaxation. The water for the baths was heated by a furnace in the cellar, where one man was responsible for maintaining the comfort level of the water. The shah made his way to the basement to visit with the man who tirelessly tended the fire.

The two men shared a meal together, and the shah befriended this lonely man. Day after day, week in and week out, the ruler went to visit the fire tender. The stranger soon became attached to his visitor because he came to where he was. No other person had showed that kind of caring or concern.

One day the shah revealed his true identity. It was a risky move, for he feared the man would ask him for special favors or for a gift. Instead, the leader's new friend looked into his eyes and said, "You left your comfortable palace and your glory to sit with me in this dungeon of darkness. You ate my bitter food and genuinely showed you cared about what happens to me. On other people you might bestow rich gifts, but to me you have given the best gift of all. You have given yourself."

For thousands of years, people have been speculating on what constitutes quality human relationships. With all the philosophies, theories, and speculations, only one principle seems to stand strong. It is not new at all. In fact, it is almost as old as history itself. It was taught in Persia over three thousand years ago by Zoroaster to his fire worshipers. Confucius asserted the principle in China twenty-four centuries ago. In the Valley of Han lived the followers of Taoism. Their leader Lao-Tzu taught the principle incessantly. Five hundred years before Christ, Buddha taught it to his

If you wish others to respect you, you must show respect for them. . . . Everyone wants to feel that he counts for something and is important to someone. Invariably, people will give their love, respect and attention to the person who fills that need. Consideration for others generally reflects faith in self and faith in others.

ARI KIEV

❋

disciples on the banks of the holy Ganges. The collections of Hinduism contained this principle over fifteen hundred years before Christ. Nineteen centuries ago, Jesus taught his disciples and followers much the same principle. He summed it up in one thought: "Do unto others as you would have them do unto you."

Unselfishly giving of ourselves probably wouldn't make it as a primary course of study in the school of success. Although we make a living by what we get, the true rewards are experienced because of what we give. You have not really lived a fulfilled day, even though you may be a success by societal standards, unless you have done something for someone who will never be able to repay you.

In the midst of your flurry of activities in this competitive, go-get-'em world, take a moment for the next several days to reflect on Rabbi Harold Kushner's thoughts: "The purpose of life is not to win. It is to grow and to share. You will get more satisfaction from the pleasure you have brought into other people's lives than you will from the times you outdid and defeated them."

A UNIQUE SPIN
ON GETTING EVEN

D uring the days of the Berlin Wall, a few East Berliners decided to send their West Berlin neighbors a "gift." They proceeded to load a dump truck with undesirables including garbage, broken bricks, building material, and any other disgusting items they could find. They calmly drove across the border, received clearance, and delivered their present by dumping it on the West Berlin side.

Needless to say, the West Berliners were irritated and intent on "getting even." People immediately began offering ideas on how to outdo the repulsive actions of their adversaries. A wise man interrupted their angry reactions and offered an entirely different approach. Surprisingly, people responded favorably to his suggestions and began loading a dump truck full of essential items scarce in East Berlin. Clothes, food, and medical supplies poured in. They drove the loaded truck across the border, carefully unloaded and

You will find as you look back on life that the moments when you have really lived are the moments when you have done things in a spirit of love.

HENRY
DRUMMOND

Shall we make a new rule of life from tonight: always to try to be a little kinder than is necessary.

JAMES M. BARRIE

stacked the precious commodities, and then left a sign that read, "Each gives according to his ability to give."

Imagine the reaction of those who saw the "payback" and powerful message on the sign. Shock. Embarrassment. Distrust. Disbelief. Maybe even a bit of regret.

What we give to others sends a loud message about who we are. How we respond to unkindness, unfairness, or ingratitude speaks a truckload about our true character.

INFLUENCE

There are little eyes upon you,
And they're watching night and day;
There are little ears that quickly
Take in every word you say;
There are little hands all eager
To do anything you do;
And a little boy who's dreaming
Of the day he'll be like you.

You're the little fellow's idol;
You're the wisest of the wise,
In his little mind about you,
No suspicions ever rise;
He believes in you devoutly,
Holds that all you say and do,
He will say and do, in your way
When he's a grown-up like you.

There's a wide-eyed little fellow,
Who believes you're always right,
And his ears are always open,
And he watches day and night;
You are setting an example
Every day in all you do,
For the little boy who's waiting
To grow up to be like you.

AUTHOR UNKNOWN

NEVER ASSUME
YOU'RE PEDALING TOGETHER

We are born for co-operation, as are the feet, the hands, the eyelids and the upper and lower jaws. People need each other to make up for what each one does not have.

MARCUS AURELIUS

❀

The definition of the word "cooperation" stems from two Latin words, *co*, meaning "with," and *opus*, meaning "work." So, quite literally, cooperation means working with others. Sounds simple, doesn't it.

For over 25 years the *Des Moines Register* newspaper has sponsored a summer RAGBRAI (Register's Annual Great Bike Ride Across Iowa). Bikers from all over the country emerge on the western side of Iowa determined to be one of hundreds of successful riders who invest a week of their life pedaling their way across the state.

One year RAGBRAI designated our community as a stopping point for the night. It was an incredible sight to watch the bikers swarm into town and set up camp. Young and old alike enjoyed the challenge, fellowship, and fun that accompanied this popular event.

As I walked through one of the camping areas, I overheard a conversation between two riders who were navigating the trail together on a tandem bike. The man was complaining about the difficulty of one of the hills they had to climb earlier in the day. "That was a struggle," he said. "I thought for sure we were going to have to push the bike up the hill on foot."

"It sure was a steep hill," his female companion responded, "and if I hadn't kept the brake on all the way, we would have rolled back down for sure."

There's practically no limit to what people can accomplish when they work cooperatively. However, if just one person drags her feet or continually applies the brake, everyone else suffers. Married couples, work departments, athletic teams, dancers, or the cast in a play need to understand where the team is going, how they will get there, what effort will be required by each person, and what they can do to help each other.

When you're on a tandem bike, you have to pedal together.

The purpose of life is to collaborate for a common cause; the problem is nobody seems to know what it is.

GERHARD GSCHWANDTNER

NO ONE IS
AN ISLAND

A true friend
never gets in
your way unless
you happen to
be going down.

ARNOLD
GLOSOW

A few years ago I conducted a seminar in Des Moines, Iowa in late October. I arose early in the morning to prepare for the program and was shocked when I turned on the television to see news reports of a premature heavy snowfall in progress. Electricity was out in various parts of the city, numerous traffic accidents had been reported, and no travel was advised.

Later in the day, the no-travel advisory had been lifted so I loaded my vehicle to attempt the trip home. On each side of the freeway that runs through Des Moines were trees loaded with the heavy white snow. I noticed in areas where evergreen trees were close together bowed branches from one tree were resting against the trunk of another, and each tree seemed to be supported by the branches or trunk of another tree.

Where trees stood alone, the heavy snow had caused tremendous damage. The branches were unable to handle the heavy weight and, without the support of other trees, they had snapped. Thousands of small and large branches painted the white landscape. Seedlings and strong mature trees were irreparably damaged.

We are not unlike those trees. When the premature, unexpected, or normal storms of life hit, we need the support of other people to withstand the weight of the burden. Human beings aren't designed to stand on their own, and the closer we grow together, the more mutual support we can provide.

FOOTSTEPS

A careful man I ought to be;
A little fellow follows me.
I do not dare to go astray
For fear he'll go the selfsame way.
Not once can I escape his eyes;
Whate'er he sees me do he tries.
Like me he says he's going to be—
That little chap who follows me.
I must remember as I go
Through summer sun and winter snow,
I'm molding for the years to be—
That little chap who follows me.

AUTHOR UNKNOWN

LOVE

There is little doubt that most of us long for stronger, more creative and rewarding ways of loving each other.

LEO F. BUSCAGLIA

GOOD ADVICE . . .
WRONG APPLICATION

Acouple engaged to be married began experiencing difficulties in their relationship. The constant conflict caused them to question their wedding plans. The man, concerned he could lose the woman he loved, realized there were many unresolved issues he had no idea how to handle. So he sought the advice of a counselor who suggested the problems could be solved if he would take up biking. "I want for you to ride ten miles a day for the next two weeks and then check back with me." Two weeks went by and the man reported back to his counselor as requested. "So, how are you and your fiancee doing now?" the counselor inquired. "How should I know," the man replied, "I'm 140 miles away from home and haven't talked to her for 14 days."

There will always be challenges and problems in any relationship. No problem! Dr. Theodore Rubin advises in *One to One*: "The problem is not that there are problems. The problem is expecting otherwise and thinking that having problems is a problem."

I like long walks, especially when they are taken by people who annoy me.

FRED ALLEN

❀

Abundant advice is available from assorted sources for anyone wishing to enrich his or her relationships. Unfortunately, none of that advice is worth a plugged nickel unless you're willing to step up your investment in people.

My advice: (1) Remember that creating and nourishing relationships is hard work; (2) there will always be problems; (3) relationships are worth every ounce of effort it takes to work through the unavoidable challenges.

This is good advice, if I must say so myself. Apply it— NOW.

CREATE YOUR EMOTIONS
THROUGH YOUR MOTIONS

D r. Joyce Brothers tells the story of a judge trying to change the mind of a woman filing for divorce. "You're 92," he said. "Your husband is 94. You've been married for 73 years. Why give up now?" "Our marriage has been on the rocks for quite a while," the woman explained, "but we decided to wait until the children died."

Dr. Robert Taylor, author of the book *Couples: The Art of Staying Together*, said, "We're now living in the age of disposability: Use it once, and throw it away. Over the past decade, there has developed a feeling that relationships are equally disposable."

The throw-away culture in which we live seems intent on throwing out the principle that marriage is a commitment requiring effort.

According to a *U.S. News and World Report* study, the single biggest reason couples split up is the "inability to talk honestly with each other, to bare their souls, and to treat each other as each other's best friend." The same factors continue to rank high on the list of reasons for marriage breakups.

Happy marriages begin when we marry the ones we love, and they blossom when we love the ones we marry

TOM MULLEN

On the dance
floor, as in life,
you're only as
good as your
partner.

ROBIN
MARANTZ
HENIG IN *USA
TODAY*

❃

Here's a familiar scenario: Your spouse complains, "You never tell me you love me anymore." You take the hint and mumble, "Of course I love you." But inside you're thinking, "Silly, I wouldn't be living with you if I didn't love you. But if anything changes, you'll be among the first to know." Why don't we just respond with a warm kiss and then say, "I'm sorry I haven't told you lately how much I love you."

The great psychologist Dr. George W. Crane said in his famous book, *Applied Psychology*, "Remember, motions are the precursors of emotions. You can't control the latter directly but only through your choice of motions or actions. . . . To avoid this all too common tragedy (marital difficulties and misunderstandings) become aware of the true psychological facts. Go through the proper motions each day and you'll soon begin to feel the corresponding emotions! Just be sure you and your mate go through those motions of dates and kisses, the phrasing of sincere daily compliments, plus the many other little courtesies and you need not worry about the emotion of love. You can't act devoted for very long without feeling devoted."

When we treat our spouse as the most important person in our life, we will begin feeling it, believing it, and enjoying it. What can you do this week to turn "motions into emotions"?

TO MY GROWN-UP SON

My hands were busy through the day
I didn't have much time to play
The little games you asked me to.
I didn't have much time for you.
I'd wash your clothes, I'd sew and cook,
But when you'd bring your picture book
And ask me please to share your fun,
I'd say: "A little later, son."
I'd tuck you in all safe at night
And hear your prayers, turn out the light,
Then tiptoe softly to the door.
I wish I'd stayed a minute more.
For life is short, the years rush past.
A little boy grows up so fast.
No longer is he at your side,
His precious secrets to confide.
The picture books are put away,
There are no longer games to play,
No good-night kiss, no prayers to hear.
That all belongs to yesteryear.
My hands, once busy, now are still.
The days are long and hard to fill.
I wish I could go back and do
The little things you asked me to.

AUTHOR UNKNOWN

WHAT DOES LOVE LOOK LIKE?

What does love look like? It has the hand to help others. It has the feet to hasten to the poor and needy. It has the eyes to see misery and want. It has the ears to hear the sighs and sorrows of men. That is what love looks like.

SAINT AUGUSTINE

Much has been written "about" love but maybe we've been short-sighted in helping people understand "how to" love. I know this is elementary, but love is more than hugs, kisses, and affection. It also transcends the emotional feeling so many consider love. Love is demonstrated by an attitude of sensitivity and concern and is expressed through sincere actions. Then, the emotion of love surfaces and grows from there.

Let me make this simple. "You can't put a price tag on love," said Melanie Clark, "but you can on all its accessories." Activating the "accessories" of love requires us to eliminate the baggage of pettiness, jealousy, resentment, and judgment. Just love. Think and behave as if you love. By loving thinking and loving actions, we expand our ability to express authentic love. Remember, the emotional part of love is achieved when the thinking and acting are activated.

Maybe a few real-life examples will clarify the "how to" for loving and encourage you to show the accessories of love:

A Welsh gentleman fell in love with one of his neighbors and wanted to marry her. The couple got into an argument and she refused to forgive. The man was shy and hesitated to face his love. Instead, he slipped a love letter under her door every week.

Finally, after 42 years, he worked up the courage, knocked on her door, and asked her to become his wife. To his surprise, she said yes. The couple was married at age 74.

Although his approach was a bit unconventional, it was a determined display of persistent love. What are you doing every week to show those you love how much they mean to you?

I've enjoyed attending the entertaining musical play *Fiddler on the Roof* many times. In one scene, Tevye, seeing the example of his daughters, begins to think about love as a basis for marriage. So after years of marriage, he asks his wife, "Do you love me?" She replies, "For 25 years I washed your clothes, slept in your bed, bore your children, and fixed your meals. If that isn't love, what is?" But Tevye persists: "Do you love me?" After repeated requests, Tevye's wife was only able to respond, "I suppose I do."

"Do you love me?" In the ideal world, this question would be unnecessary. In the real world, countless people yearn to hear the words "I love you."

Ida Fay Oblesby, writing in the *P.E.O. Record* (January 1983), tells the story of an eight-year-old girl in a Pennsylvania orphanage who was shy, unattractive, and regarded as a problem. Two other asylums had her transferred, and now this director was seeking some pretext for getting rid of her. One day, someone noticed the little girl was writing a letter. An ironclad rule of the institution was that any communication from a child had to be approved before it was mailed. The next day, the director and her assistant watched the child steal out of the dormitory and slip down to the main gate. Just inside the gate was an old tree with roots showing above the ground. They followed and watched as the child hid the letter in one of the crevices of the root. Carefully looking around, the little girl scurried back to the dormitory.

The director took the note and tore it open. Then, without speaking, she passed the note to her assistant. It read, "To anybody who finds this: I love you."

What a powerful message from the hearts of those hungry to have someone to love and love them back.

Alvin Straight lived a few miles from me in Laurens, Iowa. His brother, age 80, lived several hundred miles away in Blue River, Wisconsin. According to local news reports, Alvin's brother had suffered a stroke, and Alvin wanted to see him, but had no transportation. Alvin's eyesight wasn't good enough to have a driver's license, and he refused to take a plane, train, or bus. So Alvin, at age 73, climbed aboard his 1966 John Deere tractor lawn mower and drove it all the way to Blue River, Wisconsin. Now that's devotion.

People's needs are not inconveniences, irritations, or a disruption to our comfortable lifestyles. Needs are opportunities to share a portion of ourselves, to stretch our ability to give, and to sharpen our ability to become others-minded.

The following appeared on the editorial page of the *Pasadena Star News* in November of 1985:

Just about everyone knows the Jim Brady story—the man who, only two months after becoming White House press secretary, was shot in the head during the attempted assassination of President Reagan, and how he has fought his way back from brain surgery and the crippling, enduring damage from the stray bullet. However, not many people know, however, about the ceaseless, selfless, devoted love of Bob Dahlgren . . . a man who loved Brady like himself.

A few months ago, Bob Dahlgren died in his sleep, at 52 years of age. It didn't even make the morning news. But during the long months following the shooting, it was

Dahlgren who kept the vigil with Brady's wife, Sarah, through the long series of brain operations.

It was Dahlgren and his wife, Suzie, who took Brady's young son Scott into their home through the early days of the ordeal. It was Dahlgren who arranged the happy hours with Brady's friends by his hospital bedside. As Brady recovered and returned to a semi-normal life, it was always Dahlgren who scouted out the advance arrangements, who helped load and unload his friend from the specially equipped van in which Brady did most of his traveling. It was Dahlgren who helped Sarah field the questions about Brady's health and spent endless hours keeping friends posted on his condition. It was Dahlgren who helped organize a foundation to assure financial support for the family.

For more than four and a half years after Brady was shot, Bob Dahlgren devoted virtually all his time to the man he loved. And he did so with little recognition and no hint of seeing anything in return. Never, ever did Dahlgren complain. Never did he hesitate when needed. Never did he stop looking for the needs or the response of love.

As Dr. Arthur Kobrine, the surgeon who lived through Brady's long ordeal with him, once said, "Everyone should have a friend like Bob Dahlgren."

I read a story in *Our Daily Bread* about a king who had a silver bell placed in a high tower of his palace early in his reign. He announced that he would ring the bell whenever he was happy so that his subjects would know of his joy.

The people listened for the sound of that silver bell, but it remained silent. Days turned into weeks, and weeks into months, and months into years. But no sound of the bell rang out to indicate that the king was happy.

The king grew old and gray, and eventually he lay on his deathbed in the palace. As some of his weeping subjects gathered around him, he discovered that he had really been loved by his people all through the years. At last the king was happy. Just before he died, he reached up and pulled the rope that rang the silver bell.

Think of it—a lifetime of unhappiness because he didn't know that he was warmly loved and accepted by his loyal subjects.

Many people live out their days without the joy of knowing or experiencing the love of others. This book is filled with ideas, illustrations, and inspiration for showing others what love looks like. Give them a try.

Love is like a beautiful flower which I may not touch, but whose fragrance makes the garden a place of delight just the same.

HELEN KELLER

THE FLIP SIDE
OF LOVE

Our lives are
shaped by
those who love
us—by those
who refuse to
love us.

JOHN POWELL,
S.J.

❀

I love to watch reruns of old television series such as the *Andy Griffith Show*. Unlike many of today's programs, the oldies seem to contain a practical, life-enhancing message. In one of the first segments, Sheriff Andy Taylor decides to invite his spinster Aunt Bee to come and live with Opie and him. Following the death of his wife, Andy thought Aunt Bee would add the missing feminine touch to their home.

Opie doesn't share Andy's sentiments and is skeptical of having Aunt Bee coming to "replace" his mother. Andy devises a plan to help Opie accept the idea. He invites Aunt Bee to go fishing and frog catching with them so that Opie will have a chance to get to know her and, it's hoped, bond with her. Unfortunately, Aunt Bee fails miserably at fishing, can't catch a frog, and later reveals her lack of football skills.

Late that night, after Opie is in bed, Aunt Bee talks Andy into taking her to the bus station. Opie hears her crying beneath his bedroom window and realizes she is probably leaving. He jumps out of bed, runs downstairs and out to the truck, exclaiming, "We can't let her go, Pa; she needs us. She can't even catch frogs, take fish off the hook, or throw a football. We've got to take care of her or she'll never make it."

Love springs to life when we realize the benefit of our relationships is not what we will receive from someone else. We need other people because of our weaknesses, and they need us to complement their lives by infusing our strengths with their weaknesses. The process for creating healthy, mutually beneficial relationships unveils a realization that love is best expressed when we fill in the void in someone's life and by doing so expand the value of our own lives.

Although Sheriff Taylor acted on a pure motive of wanting a feminine touch in their home, it was Opie who delivered the punch line, "We've got to take care of her or she'll never make it." Although love may not be reciprocated by those we give it to, our lives will not remain the same when we commit to filling the vacuum in others' lives. "Love cures people," said Karl Menninger, " both the ones who give it and the ones who receive it."

Love has nothing to do with what you are expecting to get—only what you are expecting to give—which is everything. What you will receive in return varies. But it really has no connection with what you give. You give because you love and cannot help giving. If you are very lucky, you may be loved back. That is delicious but it does not necessarily happen.

KATHARINE
HEPBURN

FORGIVENESS

He that cannot forgive others
breaks the bridge over which
he must pass himself;
for every man has need to be forgiven.

THOMAS FULLER

KEEP YOUR BRIDGES
IN GOOD REPAIR

A n army general once said to John Wesley, "I never forgive and I never forget." John Wesley answered, "Then, sir, I hope you never sin."

I feel sorry for this general. He probably never experienced the load-lifting action of forgiveness. To forgive someone means to let go. Once you forgive, the emotional baggage from tension, unresolved conflicts, or mistreatment is lifted. Robin Casarjian, author of *Forgiveness: A Bold Choice for a Peaceful Heart*, who managed to forgive the man who raped her, said, "Once you forgive, you are no longer emotionally handcuffed to the person who hurt you." What freedom!

"You have a tremendous advantage over the person who slanders you or does you a willful injustice," declared Napoleon Hill. "You have it within your power to forgive that person."

Are you angry with someone who has offended you? Let it go. The anger only pulls you down. Forgiveness provides you the power to get on with life.

Do you carry grudges? Grudges are simply a buildup of resentment produced by an unwillingness to genuinely forgive. We can't "bury the hatchet" with the handle sticking out.

Have you ever said, "I'll forgive but I can't forget?" That is only superficial forgiveness allowing us to continue wallowing in self-pity. The quickest way to forget is to quit dwelling on the wrong done to you.

The American Red Cross was founded by a pioneering woman named Clara Barton, who was widely known for her forgiving spirit. On one occasion a friend brought up an injustice done to her years before. When Barton failed to respond to the effort to relive this event, the friend persisted, "Don't you remember how much that person hurt you?"

"No," Clara Barton cheerfully responded. "I distinctly remember forgetting that."

To proactively forgive the past, quit dwelling on the hurt. By not reliving the situation over and over, you will gain peace and victory over the incident.

If you want to maintain the bridges that sustain relationships but sense some repair work is needed, consider these suggestions.

1. Be the First to Ask Forgiveness. Whether you have hurt someone or been mistreated, be the first to say, "Please forgive me if I've done anything to hurt our relationship." This action will allow you to let go and get on with your life.

2. Rebuild Your Thoughts. The mind is a marvelous mechanism. The thoughts we hold in this massive human computer will dominate our lives. Although not an easy task, discipline yourself not to dwell on the situation or the bitterness, blame, or hurt that can saturate the walls of your mind.

3. Pray. I am rarely capable of genuine forgiveness without divine intervention. Relying on God to help me deal with the pain, the person, and the process of healing replaces the human tendency of revenge with release.

4. Write a Letter. Expressing your feelings in writing, without placing judgment or blame, can be a significant bridge from pain to peace. Simply communicating your heart signals a desire to achieve resolution. Whether or not you ever send the letter, writing it contains its own value.

5. Focus on the Future. Wallowing in the mire of the past destroys the bridge to the future. Tomorrow can never be lived to the fullest when we are consumed with the uncontrollable past.

Elbert Hubbard wrote, "A retentive memory may be a good thing, but the ability to forget is the true token of greatness. Successful people forget. They know the past is irrevocable. They're running a race. They can't afford to look behind. Their eye is on the finish line. Magnanimous people forget. They're too big to let little things disturb them. They forget easily. If anyone does them wrong, they consider the source and keep cool. It's only the small people who cherish revenge. Be a good forgetter. Business dictates it, and success demands it."

Forgiveness allows you to be free from the nightmares of the past and to reclaim your dreams for the future.

6. Replace Selfishness with Unconditional Love. Old Pete was in bad health and death seemed imminent. For years there had been a thorn of bitterness with Joe, formerly one of his best friends. Wanting to clear the air, Pete sent word for Joe to come and see him.

When Joe arrived, Pete told him that he couldn't live another day or face eternity knowing their relationship had been destroyed. Pete painfully and reluctantly apologized for the hurtful things he had said and done. He also assured Joe that he forgave him for his actions. The two old friends shook hands and everything seemed fine until Joe turned to go. As he turned to leave, Pete said, "If I get better, none of this counts."

Saying "I forgive you" and then placing conditions on our forgiveness equates with not forgiving at all. It's tough to remove our selfish motives and refrain from resurrecting past grievances when frictions arise.

I'm reminded of the lady who sought marriage counseling. The counselor asked her what seemed to be the source of their difficulty. "Whenever we get into an argument," the lady said, "my husband becomes historical."

"Don't you mean hysterical?" the counselor responded.

"No, I mean historical! He always brings up the past."

Emotional problems and relational stress will continue as long as forgiveness hinges on the past. Total forgiveness requires unconditional love.

I hope your relationships will continue to mature and reap positive results. A forgiving spirit is a basic requirement for that to occur. Forgiveness remains the bridge we must cross to enter brighter tomorrows. Remember the words of Martin Luther King, Jr.: "Forgiveness is not an occasional act; it is a permanent attitude."

Ninety percent of the art of living consists of getting along with people you cannot stand.
SAMUEL GOLDWYN

In *The Essential Calvin and Hobbes*, the cartoon character Calvin says to his tiger friend, Hobbes, "I feel bad that I called Susie names and hurt her feelings. I'm sorry I did it."

"Maybe you should apologize to her," Hobbes suggests.

Calvin ponders this for a moment and replies, "I keep hoping there's a less obvious solution."

There's no easy way of saying "I'm sorry, I was wrong." Do it anyway. Rather than allowing bitterness and resentment to surface, allow the sweet smell of harmony to be the trademark of your relationships.

PLACING PEOPLE
IN PROPER PERSPECTIVE

B
arbara Bush was not Wellesley College's first choice as their 1990 graduation commencement speaker. Some of the seniors were hesitant about her appropriateness as a role model for the issues facing today's modern woman.

"To honor Barbara Bush as a commencement speaker," they protested, "is to honor a woman who has gained recognition through the achievements of her husband, which contradicts what we have been taught the past four years."

The first lady handled the accusations in her normal classy style and didn't allow the protests to either offend or intimidate her. Mrs. Bush spoke from her heart and the fulfillment she had experienced from her traditional values. She offered this advice in her commencement address:

"Cherish your human connections, your relationships with friends and family. For several years, you've had impressed upon you the importance to your career of dedication and hard work.

The primary joy of life is the acceptance, approval, sense of appreciation, and companionship of our human comrades. Many men do not understand that the need for fellowship is really as deep as the need for food, and so they go throughout life accepting many substitutes for genuine, warm, simple relatedness.

JOSH
LIEBMAN

❧

"This is true, but as important as your obligations as a doctor, lawyer, or business leader will be, you are a human being first and those human connections—with spouses, with children, with friends—are the most important investments you will ever make.

"At the end of your life, you will never regret not having passed one more test, not winning one more verdict, or not closing one more deal. You will regret time not spent with a husband, a friend, a child, or a parent."

The first lady addressed the heart of living. All of our personal and professional endeavors are made sweeter, richer, and more satisfying by sharing them with others. As Antoine de Saint-Exupery wrote, "There is no joy except in human relationships."

Too often, what should matter most in our lives receives the least attention. Battles with the almighty dollar, pursuing selfish interests, attaining that next promotion, or closing a deal are empty pursuits without the human element. It's easy to overlook that our relationships are what encourage the heart and nourish the soul.

Harold Kushner, writing in *When All You've Ever Wanted Isn't Enough*, said: "A life without people, without the same people day after day, people who belong to us, people who will be there for us, people who need us and whom we need in return, may be very rich in other things, but in human terms, it is no life at all."

A life without relationships limits the value of everything you do. Regardless of the pressures you feel to succeed in our what's-in-it-for-me society, don't make the mistake of placing value on only those activities and goals that enhance your paycheck. Make time to reach out to those who add meaning to your life. And when the ties have been broken by disagreement or misunderstanding, reach out with a spirit of forgiveness.

Only you can know how much you can give to every aspect of your life. Try to decide what is the most important. And if you do, then only occasionally will you resent or regret the demands of the marriage, the career, or the child, or the staying.

BARBARA
WALTERS

BE WILLING TO SAY
"I'M SORRY"

The most deadly of all sins is the mutilation of a child's spirit.

ERIK H. ERIKSON

❋

After 15 years of being a parent, I think I'm finally realizing what I cherish most about my children: our relationship.

Oh, I admit it's nice when they score points in a basketball game or gracefully perform a dance routine. I'm pleased when their report cards reveal above-average performance or when I observe the sweat and effort put into a school project. And of course it's flattering when people comment how nice they look or how respectful they are.

But what really trips my trigger and renews my parental energy—after returning from a speaking trip, or working on a free-throw shot, playing taxi driver, or setting curfew—is a loving smile, a hug, a high five, and the four cherished words: "I love you, Dad."

I'm keenly aware how my actions, words, tone of voice, or nonverbals affect the loving, caring, and mutually respectful relationship we enjoy. And, I've failed at times as a father to uphold my end of the responsibility. There have been times when I crushed my children's spirit.

When my son was in the sixth grade, another dad and I agreed to coach a traveling basketball team. Along with our two sons, we invited ten other boys to enjoy the experience with us.

It didn't take long for me to realize that the definition of a father–coach is someone who expects his son to be everything he wasn't. I upheld high and sometimes unrealistic expectations. I even found it easy to justify my demands by attempting to motivate my son to be the best he could be. However, during one game I overstepped my parental privileges.

The game was already won. The boys fought courageously to overcome a major point deficit to hold a comfortable lead with 37 seconds left in the game. Out of nowhere Matt (my son) stole the ball, dribbled the length of the court, and MISSED an uncontested layup.

I chose to release my accumulated tension from the game on my son for missing that layup. The shot meant nothing. We had won the game and advanced to the finals. Matt played with heart and gave his all . . . yet he blew that simple layup. I let him know in no uncertain terms how disappointed I was and how ridiculous it was for him to miss such a simple shot.

The joy of winning drained from his face. He stood motionless and speechless as Dad continued to drain the power from his self-esteem battery. I knew I'd blown it but continued to justify my outburst and dig myself into a deeper hole.

It was a long and quiet few hours waiting for the championship game. Matt was hurting inside, and I was full of guilt. There was little question that I needed my son's forgiveness.

Sitting in our van outside the gymnasium, I slowly turned to look into Matt's fearful and discouraged face. "Matt, I was wrong," I began. "I'm sorry for blowing up at you. You worked hard in that game, and I failed to recognize you for all the good things you did. Please forgive me."

It was then Matt touched my heart and filled my eyes with tears. "It's okay, Dad. I know you love me."

Thanks to my son, I could walk into the championship game with a clear conscience, repaired heart, and softer spirit.

We lost the championship game by one point, but I came out of that tournament a winner. My son had forgiven me.

I realized in the van with Matt that day that I had admitted and he had acknowledged that I was human. Most important, Matt knew that I knew I was wrong and was willing to admit it.

The only way to heal a damaged spirit is to swallow the parental pride and say, "I'm sorry. I was wrong. Please forgive me." Failure to bring healing when you've been unfair or hurtful can breed anger for years to come.

If you were to ask what is the hardest task in the world, you might think of some muscular feat, some acrobatic challenge, some chore to be done on the battlefield or the playing field. Actually, there is nothing which we find more arduous than saying, "I was wrong."

SUNSHINE MAGAZINE

LET GO OF THE PAST

Forgiveness is the key that unlocks the door of resentment and the handcuffs of hate. It is a power that breaks the chains of bitterness and the shackles of selfishness.

WILLIAM ARTHUR WARD

❀

I was fairly young when the movie *The Hiding Place* was released. The impact of this dramatic story detailing one family's efforts to hide Jews in Holland from the Nazis and their later suffering in a Nazi death camp remains with me many years later. Corrie ten Boom and her family were featured in the movie, and later she returned to that death camp in Germany to deliver a message of forgiveness to a group of German people. Little did she know that this experience would test her forgiving spirit.

In her book *Tramp for the Lord*, Corrie recalls, "The place was Ravensbruck and the man who was making his way forward had been a guard—one of the most cruel guards.

"Now he was in front of me, hand thrust out: 'A fine message, Fraulein! How good it is to know that, as you say, all our sins are at the bottom of the sea!'

"And I, who had spoken so glibly of forgiveness, fumbled in my pocketbook rather than take that hand. He would not remember me, of course—how could he remember one prisoner among those thousands of women?

"But I remember him and the leather crop swinging from his belt. I was face-to-face with one of my captors and my blood seemed to freeze.

"'You mentioned Ravensbruck in your talk,' he was saying. 'I was a guard there.' No, he did not remember me.

"'But since that time,' he went on, 'I have become a Christian. I know that God has forgiven me for the cruel things I did there, but I would like to hear it from your lips as well. Fraulein'—again the hand came out—'will you forgive me?'

"And I stood there—I whose sins had again and again to be forgiven—and could not forgive. Betsie [Corrie's sister] had died in that place—could he erase her slow terrible death simply for the asking?

"It could not have been many seconds that he stood there—hand held out—but to me it seemed hours as I wrestled with the most difficult thing I had ever had to do."

Visualize that scene in your mind. Try to feel what Corrie ten Boom felt, although I doubt that any of us can come close to the inner struggle she was experiencing. How could this man expect to be forgiven for the cruel and inhumane treatment he delivered? How could he have the audacity to suggest that Corrie offer him release from his past?

Mahatma Gandhi believed that "the weak can never forgive. Forgiveness is the attribute of the strong." Corrie ten Boom was a strong person, a gallant believer in the benefits of two-way forgiveness. She forgave. I believe Corrie ten Boom not only released that prison guard from a past of regret but made a critical leap forward in her own faith, inner healing, and ability to move forward.

We all experience various ups and downs in our relationships. Some of us have been hurt by those we love the most. Others live in a daily environment of put-downs and disrespect. There are people who dread the encounter of someone who has broken their spirit and still others who shudder every time they think about people who have destroyed their trust.

Hurt people are everywhere. Relationships are in shambles. Loneliness is rampant. Undeserved unfairness, injustice, or even abandonment happens. Isolation becomes the escape for many.

There are many people out there waiting to hear the words "I forgive you," while many victims are finding a way to pay them back or seek revenge. We've become a nation obsessed with getting even. How else can you explain the headlines in our newspapers? Neighbors threatening neighbors. Lawsuits (for the most ridiculous reasons). Shootings in schools. Grudges leading to beatings. Stalkings. Parents kidnapping their own children from the other parent. The list is depressing.

Ernest Hemingway, in his short story "The Capital of the World," tells the story of a father and his teenaged son living in Spain. Through a series of events, their relationship became strained and eventually shattered. The boy opted to flee from his home, and the father began a desperate search for his lost, rebellious, yet loved son.

Running out of options, the father resorted to placing an ad in the Madrid newspaper. His son's name was Paco, a common name in Spain. The ad simply read: "Dear Paco, meet me in front of the Madrid newspaper office tomorrow at noon. All is forgiven. I love you."

Hemingway then provides us with an incredible picture and message. The next day at noon in front of the newspaper office, there were 800 "Pacos" all seeking forgiveness.

There are countless people in this world waiting to be forgiven. There are just as many who could benefit from forgiving. Show me a person who lives in peace with himself or herself and with others and I'll show you a person who freely and sincerely forgives. Forgiveness is the bridge we all must cross to leave pain, heartache, despair, anger, and hurt behind. It takes tremendous courage, humility, and a willingness to risk to cross that bridge, but on the other side peace, joy, love, and comfort await us. To fully forgive allows us to fully live.

So often people dwell on past bitterness and present themselves as a martyr for having endured. Unfortunately, the feelings of anger, mistrust, and resentment seep into their other relationships and poison what could otherwise be a healthy experience. There is only one cure and that is to forgive and let it go. Brian Tracy suggests that we "issue a blanket pardon to everyone for everything that they have ever done to hurt you in any way."

I in no way want to suggest this will be easy. In fact, Laurence Sterne said, "Only the brave know how to forgive . . . a coward never forgave; it is not in his nature." I figure if Corrie ten Boom could muster the courage to forgive the man responsible for her torment, who am I to pass eternal judgment and harbor lifelong resentment for the comparatively insignificant abuses I've experienced.

A few years ago, our high school put on the play *Joseph and the Amazing Technicolor Dreamcoat*. In addition to the enjoyment of watching my son perform on stage, I was once again reminded how this young biblical character was mistreated and hated by his brothers. Joseph was a young visionary who often had dreams about the future. What really irked his brothers is that in one dream he saw himself as ruling over his family. The brothers didn't take kindly to that. The brothers were also a bit jealous about their father's visible favoritism toward Joseph, which included the gift of a multicolored coat. Joseph's brothers figured enough is enough so they grabbed him, tossed him into a pit, and sold him into slavery.

*Doing an
injury puts you
below your
enemy;
revenging one
makes you but
even with him;
forgiving it sets
you above him.*

BENJAMIN
FRANKLIN

Joseph endured the rejection of his own blood, working for a wealthy Egyptian whose wife had a thing for Joseph and continually tried to seduce him. He was wrongly accused and imprisoned. Joseph was later released, gained favor with the king, offered power and privileges second only to the king, and was ultimately highly esteemed by others.

Here's where the story gets interesting. Years after his brothers' betrayal they came to Egypt during a time of famine looking for help from the government. Little did they know their little brother Joseph was in charge of those services. Joseph immediately recognized his brothers but it was clear to Joseph that they didn't recognize him. Joseph possessed the power to get sweet revenge, but what did he do? Joseph rose above past circumstances, refused to cast blame, and responded to his brothers in love, acceptance, and forgiveness.

Letting go of the past provides a springboard for our lives to move into the future. Corrie ten Boom did it, Joseph did it, Ronald Reagan did it, and so can you.

In *Angels Don't Die*, Patti Davis shares the impact of the attitude of her father, Ronald Reagan, had on her after the 1982 assassination attempt.

"The following day my father said he knew his physical healing was directly dependent on his ability to forgive John Hinckley. By showing me that forgiveness is the key to everything, including physical health and healing, he gave me an example of Christ-like thinking."

ACCEPTANCE

If you are losing a tug-of-war with a tiger,
give him the rope before he gets to your arm.
You can always buy a new rope.

MAX GUNTHER

MY WIFE IS ALWAYS RIGHT

A message on my desk indicated that my wife had called while I was in an early-morning meeting. The note stated I was to call her as soon as possible.

Marty rarely calls me at work. She's made it a habit not to interrupt my day unless there is an emergency or an issue needing immediate attention. As a result, I was a bit anxious returning her call.

"Hello, sweetheart," I said. "What's up?"

"A bad thing happened," she sheepishly replied. "You know, it's really noisy when you back your car into the garage door."

"Pardon me," I responded while quickly attempting to visualize the scene.

"It's your fault," she continued. "When you left for work this morning, you left your garage door open. I entered the garage through your open door, and the garage was so well lit from the outside light I didn't realize my door was closed."

"It's my fault?" I chuckled.

"Yes, and now the door is shattered."

Marty and I have laughed about that situation many times, and I, of course, continue to remind her that I was not the one in the driver's seat. However, I learned a few important things about potential conflicts, arguments, and marital disputes from this unfortunate incident. First, scratched bumpers and dented trunks can be fixed. They are not worth getting upset about, especially at the expense of harmony.

Second (and this is most important), I learned that my wife is always right. Now don't get me wrong here. I don't mean to say that I am always wrong, but I carefully choose the issues worth debating. I often recall the advice of Jonathan Kozol: "Pick battles big enough to matter, small enough to win." In other words, decide what issues are worth dying for and which ones you refuse to argue about.

The newspaper and magazine editor H. L. Mencken often drew letters of criticism and outrage for his critiques of American life. He answered every critical letter and handled each one the same way. Mencken simply wrote back, "You may be right." What a marvelous way to diffuse a potentially volatile situation.

For most of us the hardest thing to give is . . . "giving in." Wanting to win fuels the fire and often causes arguments to digress into a lose–lose situation. Maybe that's why Ben Franklin believed, "If you argue and rankle and contradict, you may achieve a victory sometimes; but it will be an empty victory because you will never get your opponent's good will."

Franklin's comment reminds me of the couple traveling down the highway in complete silence. An earlier argument left both unwilling to concede their positions. Passing a barnyard of mules, the husband sarcastically asked, "Are they relatives of yours?"

"Yes," his wife replied. "I married into the family." Ouch!

Sydney J. Harris submitted, "The most important thing in an argument, next to being right, is to leave an escape hatch for your opponent, so that he can gracefully swing over to your side without too much apparent loss of face." That's why I've adopted the attitude that my wife (and other potential opponents) are always right, even though in the long run my conviction might be proven right.

What's the benefit of taking such an approach? Isn't this a chicken way out? I suppose you could look at it like that.

Even though I know there are two sides to every issue—my side and the side that no informed, intelligent, clear-thinking, self-respecting person could possibly hold (only kidding)—any quarrel will not last long if we refuse to continue stirring it up by trying to prove others wrong.

The story is told about two guys, Jake and Sam, who were stuck together on a deserted island. They got along so well that not even a cross word passed between them. In fact, their passive behavior made life so harmonious that it became monotonous at times.

One day Jake came up with an idea to break the boredom. "Let's have a heated argument," he suggested, "like people back home often have." Sam responded, "But we don't have anything to argue about." Jake thought for a moment and then suggested, "Let's find a bottle that's washed up on shore and place it on the beach between us. I'll say, 'This bottle is mine!' And you'll say, 'No, it isn't, the bottle is mine!' That will surely get a good argument started."

So, finding a bottle and placing it on the sandy beach between them, Jake exclaimed, "This bottle is mine!" Sam, pausing a moment, responded meekly, "I think, my friend, that the bottle is mine." "Oh, really," Jake said agreeably, "if the bottle is yours, take it."

It is not humanly possible to carry on an argument between two people when one refuses to argue. So, here's a thought: Let people be right until the heat has subsided and you can discuss the situation rationally.

Two months after our car crashed into the garage door and we had purchased a minivan with a luggage carrier (don't get ahead of me), I got another call at work. "Glenn, you closed your door but my garage door didn't go up high enough so the luggage carrier hooked the garage door and shattered it. The luggage carrier isn't in such good shape either."

You can draw your own conclusions on how this conversation ended.

Over the years I've come to know that there are times when it is best to simply accept my wife's point of view, especially at times when emotions can run high (like after the second garage-door mishap). I know that I can always broach the subject later and rationally discuss the situation. What almost invariably happens is that later, when we're both feeling more rational, we're not interested in who was at fault. What seemed like a major issue earlier suddenly doesn't seem so important, and what may have ended in a disagreement is now a calm discussion without mention of who's wrong or right.

A married couple were involved in another round of repeated disagreements. The same issue had been bitterly discussed over and over. The wife finally blurted in desperation, "You're impossible!"

Not missing a beat, the husband retorted, "No, I'm next to impossible."

CREATING A RELATIONSHIP
MASTERPIECE

A relationship is a living thing. It needs and benefits from the same attention to detail that an artist lavishes on his art.

DAVID
VISCOTT

❁

L et's carry David Viscott's artistic thought a bit further. Consider the following qualities present in relationship masterpieces.

Start with a blank canvas of acceptance. Permit people to be who they are—not what they could be, should be, or would be if only they listened to you. Accept the imperfections and celebrate each person's individuality. Acceptance affirms people's value, raises self-esteem, and makes them feel comfortable in your presence.

Artists are masters at the use of primary colors, which create the heart of the finished product. Mutual trust is one such primary ingredient. We live in an imperfect, messy world made up of imperfect people. Unfortunately, many of us are prone to trusting people when they prove themselves trustworthy. I tend to believe that if we trust people, they will prove themselves trustworthy. I know trust can be betrayed but it is essential for relationships to develop. Step out. Make an effort to believe in the intrinsic goodness of people. Sure you might be disappointed at times, but you will also be blessed.

Share yourself with others. There is a bit of risk here but withholding who we are places a permanent blemish on the relationship canvas. Open and honest communication stands out in any close friendship. Use discretion but share your hurts, fears, and failures. Throw the good stuff in there too. Just refrain from unnecessary critical, cheap shots or hurting comments that are better left unsaid.

I'm sure every artist has his or her favorite color that tends to find its way into each creation. My favorite relationship ingredient is improving the ability to see the good in people. Tell your friends, family, and coworkers what you like about them. Tell people how thankful you are for them. Recognize their talents, applaud their successes (one of the most difficult actions of human nature), and make others feel important about themselves. Expressing appreciation on every possible occasion is one of the surest ways to boost mutual respect and encourage positive behaviors.

A masterpiece stands out in the viewer's mind when the proper highlights are added. When it comes to relationships, you can move to the next level by:

Giving more than you get

Allowing people to have their space

Maintaining confidentiality

Giving supportive and positive advice

Being loyal

Listening

Treating others with dignity

Saying "please" and "thank you"

Being agreeable

Accepting others' opinions

Forgiving wrongs committed

Quality relationships are most fulfilling. Relationships don't fail to become a beautiful experience because they are wrong but because most people don't want to invest what it takes to create an original. To evaluate how effective you are in creating a relationship masterpiece, just ask yourself, "If I were my friend, would I enjoy the artistic strokes (qualities) I experience being with me?"

LOYALTY

I'm very loyal in a
relationship.
When I go out with my mom,
I don't look at other moms.
I don't go, "Oooh, I wonder
what her macaroni and cheese
tastes like."

GARY SHANDLING

SHE COULD HAVE
MARRIED MOZART

At the heart of personality is the need to feel a sense of being lovable without having to qualify for that acceptance.

MAURICE
WAGNER

❋

Joe was a little shy in his teenage years, and even in college he found it difficult to ask girls out on dates. One night a buddy, Jake, who lived down the hall from Joe in the same dormitory presented an offer he couldn't refuse. "I've got great news," Jake began. "I've lined you up with a great date for Saturday night. Everything is set."

"Who is it?" Joe asked. It turned out to be a friend of Jake's girlfriend, who was going to be visiting for the weekend. Joe had never met her. "No, thank you," Joe said. "Blind dates aren't for me."

"No need to worry about this one," Jake reassured Joe. "Julie's a terrific girl. And trust me—she's a beauty."

"No," Joe repeated.

"This is a no-fail situation. I'll even give you an out."

Now he had Joe's attention. "How?" Joe asked.

"When we get to the dorm room to pick them up, wait for her to come to the door and check her out. If you like what you see, then great, we're off for a super evening. But if she's ugly, fake an asthma attack. Just go 'Aaahhhgggggg!' and grab your throat as if you're having trouble breathing. When she asks, 'What's wrong?' you say, 'It's my asthma.' And so we'll call off the date. Just like that. No questions asked. No problem."

Joe was hesitant, to say the least, but agreed to give it a try. What did he have to lose?

When they got to the door, Joe knocked and she came to the door. He took one look at her and couldn't believe his eyes. She was beautiful. How lucky could he get? He hardly knew what to say.

She took one look at Joe and went, "Aaahhhhgggggg!"

It seems they weren't the only ones with a foolproof plan. Most of us, at one time or another, have been rejected by someone because we weren't smart enough, tall enough, athletic enough, good looking enough, or whatever. It's tough to feel rejected.

When we unconditionally accept someone, we give them the freedom to be on the outside who they are on the inside. True acceptance will allow us to see the real value of a human being.

The young woman who was engaged to Mozart, before he rose to fame, could have benefited from a spirit of unconditional acceptance. Impressed by more handsome men, she became disenchanted with him because he was so short. She ultimately gave him up for someone tall and attractive. When the world began to recognize Mozart for his outstanding musical accomplishments, she regretted her decision. "I knew nothing of the greatness of his genius," she said. "I only saw him as a little man."

Acceptance communicates love and value and gives people the self-confidence to become all they can be. It also allows them to be who they are until they become what they are capable of becoming.

When Marty and I were dating, I knew we were going to have a wonderful future together. If she would only make a few changes that future could be even brighter. I'm not naive, so I certainly didn't bring up the issue during our dating and refrained from talking about it on our honeymoon.

Within a few weeks of settling into marital bliss, I decided it was time to bring my suggested changes to the surface. I was bold and stupid enough to verbalize my thoughts at supper one night. I gracefully, lovingly, and rather forthrightly stated my case. Wow, did I learn a ton about marriage that night. I also gleaned a valuable lesson about acceptance.

When we attempt to force people to be who we want them to be, the defensive, stubborn, and hurt qualities emerge. However, when you allow people to refuse to change, you give them the freedom to change.

Refrain from accepting people based on what they could be, should be, or would be if only they listened to you. Until we accept unconditionally, we will continually be looking through the filters of musts, shoulds, ought-to's, have-to's, and prejudices.

Eugene Kennedy suggests that, "When someone prizes us just as we are, he or she confirms our existence." After being married over 20 years I'm realizing the value of loving someone regardless of who they are or aren't, what they have or don't have, or for what they do or don't do.

I love the *Peanuts* cartoon where Lucy says to Snoopy:

"There are times when you really bug me, but I must admit there are also times when I feel like giving you a big hug."

Snoopy replies:

"That's the way I am . . . huggable and buggable."

Seems to me that might be an appropriate description for most people in this world . . . huggable and buggable. Love them anyway.

Here's a flash of insight from Newsweek magazine. According to reported research, the spotted owl's greatest threat may not be logging, but one of its relatives.

For the past several years, the barred owl has been rapidly migrating westward. Barred owls, which used to live exclusively east of the Mississippi, enjoy the same food as spotted owls but are more aggressive and adaptable.

Sometimes, even our relatives (whom we can't choose) cause us the most difficulty. It's then we need a good friend who won't fight us but will participate with us in the things we both enjoy.

I HAVE A PROPOSITION
FOR YOU

I n my senior year of college I took a class entitled "Marriage and the Family." I wasn't even dating anyone at the time but I figured why not prepare for future possibilities. The professor was an entertaining person and offered ample personal examples from his marriage to liven up the lecture. At the time, I questioned the validity of his stories but now that I've been married 25 years I understand how even the most outlandish ones could be true.

Whoever thinks marriage is a 50–50 proposition doesn't know the half of it.

FRANKLIN P. JONES

He began his lecture one day with this bold statement: "The secret of a successful marriage is this: Marriage is not a 50–50 proposition. A 50–50 proposition is one where nobody is giving anything.

"Rather, the secret of a happy marriage is 60–40. The husband gives in 60 percent of the time and expects his wife to give in 40 percent of the time. The wife gives in 60 percent of the time and expects her husband to give in 40 percent of the time. In a 60–40 proposition, you don't clash in the middle and say, 'Now, it's your turn.' Instead, you intersect and overlap, because you're each giving 60 percent."

I walked out of that classroom, along with 75 other students, and never thought about the 60–40 proposition again, except of course when it appeared on the final exam. I'm not sure there is any magic formula for successful marriage, but I remain intrigued by the concept of always giving a little more than the other person. There is some truth in the saying that "marriage is an empty box. It remains empty unless you put more in than you take out."

There are no doubt a multitude of attitudes, abilities, and opinions about what makes a marriage work. In fact, I've pulled together a few tidbits of marriage wisdom. I thought you might enjoy a wide spectrum of perspectives on the joys of tying the knot. Some of the ideas reflect marvelous wisdom while others are intended to offer a bit of levity.

The difference between a successful marriage and a mediocre one consists of leaving about three things a day unsaid.

MICHELLE GELMAN

The failure of modern marriage is, in large measure,
accounted for by our failure to employ humor in the process
of marital adjustment.

JULIUS GORDON

Only two things are necessary to keep one's wife happy. First
is to let her think she's having her own way. Second is to let
her have it.

LADY BIRD JOHNSON

Marriage is not just spiritual communion and passionate
embraces; marriage is also three-meals-a-day and
remembering to carry out the trash.

DR. JOYCE BROTHERS

A happy wife sometimes has the best husband, but more
often makes the best of the husband she has.

MARK BELTAIRE

It takes a loose rein to keep a marriage tight.

JOHN STEVENSON

Marriage is popular because it combines the maximum of
temptation with the maximum of opportunity.

GEORGE BERNARD SHAW

Marriage resembles a pair of shears, so joined that they cannot be separated; often moving in opposite directions, yet always punishing anyone who comes between them.

SYDNEY SMITH

Marriage should be a duet—when one sings, the other claps.

JOE MURRAY

I've never thought about divorce. I've thought about murder, but never divorce.

DR. JOYCE BROTHERS

Marriage is a lot like taking vitamins. It's a process that involves the supplementation of each other's minimum daily requirements.

PAUL NEWMAN

Sometimes I wonder if men and women really suit each other. Perhaps they should live next door and just visit now and then.

KATHARINE HEPBURN

One of the reasons I made the most important decision of my life—to marry George Bush—is because he made me laugh. It's true, sometimes we laugh through our tears, but that shared laughter has been one of our strongest bonds.

BARBARA BUSH

There is no more lovely, friendly and charming relationship, communion or company than a good marriage.

MARTIN LUTHER

People are always asking couples whose marriage has endured at least a quarter of a century for their secret for success. Actually, it is no secret at all. I am a forgiving woman. Long ago, I forgave my husband for not being Paul Newman.

ERMA BOMBECK

Lots of people have asked me what Gracie and I did to make our marriage work. It's simple—we didn't do anything. I think the trouble with a lot of people is that they work too hard at staying married. They make a business out of it. When you work too hard at a business, you get tired; and when you get tired, you get grouchy; and when you get grouchy, you start fighting; and when you start fighting, you're out of business.

GEORGE BURNS

An archaeologist is the best husband any woman can have. The older she gets, the more he is interested in her!

AGATHA CHRISTIE

Some people ask the secret of our long marriage. We take time to go to a restaurant two times a week. A little candlelight, dinner, soft music and dancing. She goes Tuesdays. I go Fridays.

HENNY YOUNGMAN

We have a picture of the perfect partner, but we marry an imperfect person. Then we have two options. Tear up the picture and accept the person, or tear up the person and accept the picture.

J. GRANT HOWARD, JR.

It destroys one's nerves to be amiable every day to the same human being.

BENJAMIN DISRAELI

Familiarity breeds contempt—and children.

MARK TWAIN

The most important thing a father can do for his children is to love their mother.

REV. THEODORE HESBURGH

More marriages might survive if the partners realized that sometimes the better comes after the worse.

DOUG LARSON

After winning an argument with his wife, the wisest thing a man can do is apologize.

ANN LANDERS

We sleep in separate rooms; we have dinner apart; we take separate vacations—we're doing everything we can to keep our marriage together.

RODNEY DANGERFIELD

And finally from the 1763 King of Poland, Stanislaus Leszcynski:

In marrying, you vow to love one another. Would it not be better for your happiness if you vowed to please one another.

UNDERSTANDING

If I can listen to what he tells me, if I can understand how it seems to him, if I can sense the emotional flavor which it has for him, then I will be releasing potent forces of change within him.

CARL ROGERS

WHOSE LANGUAGE ARE YOU SPEAKING?

D r. Robert Schuller, in his book *Reach Out for New Life*, tells a story about an incident that occurred many years ago in England. The character at the heart of the story was the most famous elephant in the circus world named Bozo.

Bozo was a beautiful beast—a great big tender hunk of gentleness. Children would come to the circus and extend their open palms, filled with peanuts, through the gate. The elephant would extend his trunk to pick the peanuts out of their hands and then curl his trunk and feed himself. He seemed to smile as he swallowed the gifts. Everyone loved Bozo.

Then one day something happened that changed his personality from positive to negative almost overnight. He almost stampeded, threatening to crush the man who was cleaning his cage. Then he began to charge the children. The circus owner knew the elephant was now dangerous and that the problem had to be faced. He came to the conclusion that he would have to exterminate this big old beast. This decision hurt him, first, because he loved the elephant; second, because it was the only elephant he had. Bozo had been imported from India, and it would cost him thousands of dollars to replace him.

Then he had an idea. This desperate and crude man decided that he would sell tickets to view the execution of Bozo. At least he would be able to raise the money to replace him.

The story spread, tickets were sold out, and the place was jammed. There, on the appointed date, was Bozo in his cage, as three men with high-powered rifles rose to take aim at the great beast's head.

Just before the signal to shoot, a little stubby man with a brown derby hat stepped out of the crowd, walked over to the owner, and said, "Sir, this is not necessary. This is not a bad elephant." The owner said, "But it is. We must kill him before he kills someone." The little man with the derby hat said, "Sir, give me two minutes alone in his cage, and I'll prove that you are wrong. He is not a bad elephant."

The circus owner thought for a moment, wrung his hands and said, "All right. But first you must sign a note absolving me of all responsibility if you get killed."

The little man scribbled on a piece of paper the words "I absolve you of all guilt," signed his name, folded the paper, and handed it to the circus owner. The owner opened the door to the cage. The little man threw his brown derby hat on the ground and stepped into the cage. As soon as he was inside, the door was locked behind him. The elephant raised his trunk and bellowed and trumpeted loudly.

But before the elephant could charge, the little man began talking to him, looking him straight in the eye. The people close by could hear the little man talking, but they couldn't understand what he was saying. It seemed as if he were speaking in an unknown tongue. The elephant still trembled, but hearing these strange words from this little man he began to whine, cry, and wave his head back and forth. The stranger walked up to Bozo and began to stroke his trunk. The now gentle beast tenderly wrapped his trunk around the feet of the little man, lifted him up, carried him around his cage, and cautiously put him back down at the door. Everyone applauded.

As he walked out of the cage, the little man said to the keeper, "You see? He is a good elephant. His only problem is that he is an Indian elephant, and he only understands

Hindustani. He was homesick for someone who could understand him. I suggest, sir, that you find someone in London who speaks Hindustani and have him come in and just talk to the elephant. You'll have no problems."

As the man picked up his derby and walked away, the circus owner looked at the note and read the signature of the man who had signed it. The man with the little brown derby was Rudyard Kipling.

Dr. Schuller said, "People also become frustrated, angry, and defeated when no one understands them." Could it be the person you are having a difficult time with just needs someone to understand their situation, to speak their language.

John Luther believed, "Natural talent, intelligence, a wonderful education—none of these guarantees success. Something else is needed: The sensitivity to understand what other people want and the willingness to give it to them."

PEOPLE DO THINGS
FOR THEIR REASONS

I think Mark Twain must have had a bad day when this quote was recorded. Although there is good reason for the common theory that a dog is man's best friend, even a dog can become disillusioned if the relationship is a one-way affair. Let me explain what I mean.

Ralph Waldo Emerson was a great historian, poet, and philosopher, but he didn't know much about getting a stubborn calf through a barn door. One day, Emerson and his son were involved in such a challenge. Can't you just see the son with his arms around the calf's neck and Emerson in the rear braced to push with all his might? As they pushed and pulled repeatedly, the calf braced itself by locking her knees and digging her feet into the ground determined not to comply.

Drenched with sweat, full of bovine smell, and frustrated to the point of exasperation, Emerson stood helpless over the calf. An Irish servant girl who had observed

If you pick up a starving dog and make him prosperous, he will not bite you. This is the principal difference between a man and a dog.

MARK TWAIN

the comical pursuit approached Emerson and asked if she could be of assistance. She walked around to the front of the calf and thrust her finger in the calf's mouth, and the calf peacefully followed the girl into the barn.

Bob Conklin, in *How to Get People to Do Things*, said, "People are like that calf. You can poke them, prod them, push them, and they don't move. But give them a good reason— one of their reasons—a way in which they will benefit, and they will follow gently along. People will do things for *their* reasons. Not *your* reasons. And those reasons are emotional, aroused by the way they feel."

People do things for their reasons, not your reasons. This is one of the greatest and yet simplest principles of human relations. People do things because they want to, not because you want them to. As Lord Chesterfield advised, "If you will please people, you must please them in their own way."

Once we understand that relationships evolve around people's needs and expectations, it's more natural to create an environment where mutual warmth and love exist.

What do people need? What are the reasons people do things? What are the qualities we display that cause people to want to pursue and maintain a relationship with us?

Don't make this too philosophical or difficult. In many ways, Anthony Robbins's comment that "When people are like each other, they tend to like each other" provides us a hint to the answers we're looking for. The same things that cause you to be drawn to someone oftentimes open the door for others to feel comfortable with you.

Make a list of the qualities, actions, and attitudes of people you enjoy being around. Endeavor to sharpen and refine those attributes in your life. There is no shortcut to nourishing relationships, but understanding what people need is the shortest way between where you are and where you want your relationships to be.

To counter Mark Twain's cynical comparison between people and dogs, perhaps we should consider that oftentimes we give more thought and energy to what our dog wants and likes than we do to our spouse, children, and friends.

Needing someone is like needing a parachute. If he isn't there the first time you need him, chances are you won't be needing him again.

DILBERT'S WORDS OF WISDOM

COULD YOU
JUST LISTEN?

*Most of the
successful
people I've
known are ones
who do more
listening than
talking. If you
choose your
company
carefully, it's
worth listening
to what they
have to say.
You don't have
to blow out the
other fellow's
light to let
your own
shine.*

BERNARD M.
BARUCH

It happens about once a week. My wife and I have a nice conversation about a favorite topic, or she will fill me in on the details of an upcoming event. A little while later I ask a question that she already addressed in our conversation. Marty then looks at me and says, "You never listen to me." Ouch. I do listen, I think, but for some reason a portion of the information just seems to leak from my memory. Although I think I know how to listen, my actions often prove otherwise.

John Maxwell tells a delightful story about an 89-year-old woman with hearing problems. She visited her doctor, and after examining her, he said, "We now have a procedure that can correct your hearing problem. When would you like to schedule the operation?"

"There won't be any operation because I don't want my hearing corrected," said the woman. "I'm 89 years old, and I've heard enough!"

There are times, at any age, where we might think "I've heard enough and don't care to listen anymore." Karl

Menninger believes, "The friends who listen to us are the ones we move toward, and we want to sit in their radius." If a relationship is important to us, it's wise to remember that the difference between someone feeling comfortable with us or avoiding us often depends on our willingness to listen.

The following poem reveals the feelings of someone who badly wants to be heard.

> When I ask you to listen to me
> and you start giving me advice,
> you have not done what I asked.
>
> When I ask you to listen to me
> and you tell me I shouldn't feel that way,
> you are trampling on my feelings.
>
> When I ask you to listen to me
> and you try to solve my problems for me,
> you have failed me.
>
> Listen! All I asked was that you listen,
> not talk to or do—
> just hear me.
>
> Advice is cheap;
> the price of a newspaper will get you both
> Dear Abby and Billy Graham.

I can do for myself; I'm not helpless—
maybe discouraged and faltering
but not helpless.

So please listen and just hear me.

And if you want to talk,
wait a minute for your turn—
and I'll listen to you.

AUTHOR UNKNOWN

This unknown writer was expressing a frustration experienced by a multitude of people everyday. From the corporate office to the school playground, from the hospital room to the bedroom, and from the subway to the carpool you will find people who genuinely feel no one is interested in their life. Paul Tournier addressed this universal need. "It is impossible," he said, "to overemphasize the immense need humans have to be really listened to, to be taken seriously, to be understood. No one can develop freely in this world and find their life full, without feeling understood by at least one person. . . Listen to all the conversations of our world, between nations as well as between couples. They are for the most part, dialogues of the deaf."

Studies indicate that we spend 30 percent of a normal business day speaking, 16 percent reading, 9 percent writing, and 45 percent, the majority of our time, listening. Yet, very few people have studied or mastered listening techniques even though close to half of our day is spent in such activity.

An unofficial listening study offers this perspective: "We hear half of what is being said, listen to half of what we hear, understand half of it, believe half of that and remember only half of that." If you translate those assumptions into an eight-hour workday, it means that:

You spend about four hours in listening activities;

You hear about two hours' worth;

You actually listen to an hour's worth;

You understand 30 minutes of that hour;

You believe only 15 minutes' worth; and

You remember just under 8 minutes' worth.

Listening is primarily an activity of the mind, not the ear. When the mind is not actively involved in the process, it should be called hearing, not listening.

MORTIMER ADLER

Statistics indicate the importance and difficulty of listening as well as the widespread listening incompetence most people display. The world needs people who aspire to be listeners. Ironically, they not only enhance others' lives but their own as well. It is a win–win affair. And, the benefits of acquiring this important skill are enjoyed throughout our lives.

PLEASE UNDERSTAND ME

A few weeks into my daughter's freshman year of high school, she became frustrated. Although a normally happy, vivacious young lady, the pressures of school, conflict with friends, teacher expectations, and the time demands of extracurricular activities were a bit over-whelming. As Katy shared her traumatic experiences with me, I tried to console her by telling her everything would be okay and that she need not be distressed by these minor difficulties.

"That's easy for you to say, Dad," she responded. "You have all your problems over with."

From a teenager's perspective adults are all through with their problems and life is one continuous party. Even more important, I think Katy was trying to tell me she could use a little empathy. She wanted me to understand what it feels like to be a freshman. I gave my daughter sound, practical, and realistic advice when all she really wanted was an understanding heart. This could have been a magical father–daughter moment. Instead, it was just another conversation.

To love you as I love myself is to seek to hear you as I want to be heard and understand you as I long to be understood.

DAVID
AUGSBURGER

Poet Shel Silverstein wrote a heart-touching verse entitled "The Little Boy and the Old Man." In it he portrays a young boy talking to an elderly gentleman.

The boy says, "Sometimes I drop my spoon." "I do that too," replies the old man.

"I often cry," continues the boy. The old man nods, "So do I."

"But worst of all," says the boy, "it seems grownups don't pay attention to me." Just then the boy feels "the warmth of a wrinkled hand." "I know what you mean," says the little old man.

Most people think they see the world as it is. Unfortunately, we really see the world as we are.

I saw my daughter's difficulties through the eyes of a grownup, not a high school freshman. The little boy saw the world through his eyes, which he learned were much like the eyes of the old man. In a world obsessed with "me" there is a tremendous opportunity to touch people's lives by focusing on what's important to them.

John Powell wrote, "Sometimes I think that the main obstacle to empathy is our persistent belief that everybody is exactly like us." I know that doesn't sound too profound but the significance of that statement is an entryway to people's hearts. To realize others don't necessarily think like me, act like me, feel as I feel, or respond to every situation as I would respond prepares me to gain valuable insights that might otherwise have been overlooked.

The ability to truly understand other people is a valuable asset. It involves opening your mind and heart with an insatiable desire to help people feel understood. A sincere attempt is made in every conversation to think how others think and feel what others are feeling. If every conversation began and evolved around this intent, I wonder how many conflicts could be avoided.

Are your daily conversations motivated by a desire to get people to understand you, or are you committed in every conversation to put yourself in the other person's world? See her world, experiences, hopes, fears, and dreams as she sees them. The benefits are immeasurable because for every person we sincerely seek to understand, there will be someone who wants to do the same for us.

Make it possible for someone today to say, "When I'm with you, I feel understood."

Sometimes you can defuse a difficult situation simply by being willing to understand the other person. Often all that people need is to know that someone else cares about how they feel and is attempting to understand their position.
BRIAN TRACY

ENCOURAGEMENT

*You can't make the other fellow feel
important in your presence if you secretly
feel that he is a nobody.*

LES GIBLIN

HOW GOOD CAN
PEOPLE BE?

I read about a young football coach at Louisiana State University who knew how to capitalize on high expectations. Paul Dietzel's 1958 football team was picked to finish near the bottom of the Southeastern Conference. Of his top 30 players, none of them weighed over 210 pounds and their abilities were far from impressive. Dietzel eliminated the customary first-, second-, and third-team concept and, instead, broke his squad into three units and named them the White Team, Go Team, and Chinese Bandits. The Chinese Bandit squad would customarily be known as benchwarmers. However, Dietzel convinced them they were defensive specialists and challenged them to live up to their name.

Throughout the season, the Chinese Bandits were called upon to display their tough and aggressive defensive tactics that frequently spelled the difference between winning and losing. That year, L.S.U. defied all odds by going undefeated

The only person who behaves sensibly is my tailor. He takes new measurements every time he sees me. All the rest go on with their old measurements.

GEORGE
BERNARD
SHAW

❀

and being named the number-one team in both the Associated Press and United Press polls.

The 1958 L.S.U. football team wasn't technically very good, but Dietzel never let them know it. He wasn't like the football coach who told his team, "We are undefeated and untied. Nobody has scored on us. Enjoy it because we now have to play our first game." Dietzel instilled a belief in his players that they could succeed and that belief produced the power to live up to his expectations.

How good would you be if you didn't know how good you were? How good would your team be if they didn't know how good they were? How good could those around you become if you raised your expectations of them?

Create high expectations for people and let them know you believe in them more than they believe in themselves. People succeed if someone they respect thinks they can.

OFFER A SHOULDER
TO LEAN ON

The 1992 Olympics in Barcelona, Spain provided spectators with a multitude of great moments. Reruns of one track-and-field event live in my memory.

Britain's Derek Redmond had a lifelong dream of winning a gold medal in the 400-meter race. His chances of achieving that dream increased when the gun sounded to begin the semifinals in Barcelona. Redmond was running a great race, and the finish line was clearly in sight as he rounded the turn in the backstretch. Then disaster struck. A sharp pain shot up the back of his leg. He fell face-first onto the track with a torn right hamstring.

Sports Illustrated provided this account of the events that followed:

As the medical attendants were approaching, Redmond fought to his feet. "It was animal instinct," he would say later. He set out hopping, in a crazed attempt to finish the race.

Few things in the world are more powerful than a positive push. A smile. A word of optimism and hope. A 'you can do it' when things are tough.

RICHARD M. DEVOS

When he reached the stretch, a large man in a T-shirt came out of the stands, hurled aside a security guard and ran to Redmond, embracing him. It was Jim Redmond, Derek's father. "You don't have to do this," he told his weeping son. "Yes, I do," said Derek. "Well, then," said Jim, "we're going to finish this together."

And they did. Fighting off security men, the son's head sometimes buried in his father's shoulder, they stayed in Derek's lane all the way to the end, as the crowd gaped, then rose and howled and wept.

What a dramatic sight! Derek Redmond failed to capture a gold medal, but he left Barcelona with an incredible memory of a father who left the crowd to share his son's pain. Together, they limped to the finish.

There isn't a person alive who hasn't experienced the disappointment of unmet expectations. Things don't always go as planned in the pursuit of our dreams. Unexpected obstacles, unplanned events, or the onset of circumstances beyond our control can burst our bubble. It is amazing how quickly our hopes can vanish followed by the pangs of failure, embarrassment, and discouragement.

A word of encouragement during a failure is worth more than a whole load of praise after a success. Orison Swett

Marden said, "There is no medicine like hope, no incentive so great, and no tonics so powerful as expectation of something better tomorrow." You can be the distributor of hope that propels someone past the present burden and into future possibilities.

Understanding how quickly momentum can be brought to an abrupt halt increases our sensitivity to how others feel when disappointments sabotage their dreams. It's then that people need someone who cares enough about them to come out of the crowd and on to the track. Let them know you are there for them. Offer a shoulder to lean on to help carry them through the pain. They may not attain the level of success they aspired to, but they'll never forget the person who lifted them up when they felt let down.

The worst part of success is trying to find someone who is happy for you.
BETTE
MIDLER

HELP PEOPLE BELIEVE
IN THEMSELVES

Those who
believe in our
ability do more
than stimulate
us. They create
for us an
atmosphere in
which it
becomes easier
to succeed.

JOHN H.
SPALDING

❄

ogi Berra was asked whether he thought Don Mattingly's performance in 1984 exceeded his expectations. Yogi responded, "No, but he did a lot better than I thought he would."

Yogi Berra is a master of confusing messages. Yet, our message concerning what we expect of others is normally received loud and clear.

Tommy was having a difficult time in school. He was full of questions and tended to fall behind on class assignments. Tommy's teacher became frustrated with his performance and told his mother Tommy had little chance for academic achievement or life success.

Tommy's mother believed differently. She removed Tommy from the low-expectation environment and taught him herself. She nurtured his inquisitive nature and encouraged him to use failure as a signal to find another way.

Tommy did all right for himself. He became an inventor, recording more than a thousand patents. We can thank him for the lights in our homes and countless other electronic inventions. Thomas Edison thrived on the hope created by his mother's positive expectations.

Our mission in relationships should not be to impress others but to get people to believe in themselves. When we express faith, the door is opened for people to think higher of themselves. That confidence in themselves creates an environment in which people feel safe to risk going beyond where they are. Every time you express positive expectations in someone, you're providing life-sustaining nutrition.

Rent the movie *Stand and Deliver*. Watch how calculus teacher Jaime Escalante works with high-school students in East Los Angeles. Keep in mind this is a part of the country where high expectations are virtually nonexistent, and the idea of quality education is a hopeless pursuit.

Escalante endeavors to work with his students to exceed all previous societal and self-imposed limitations. He's committed to offering them an opportunity to believe in themselves and create hope for the future. The kids respond.

Keep away from people who try to belittle your ambitions. Small people always do that, but the really great make you feel that you, too, can become great.

MARK TWAIN

❀

I smiled when the Educational Testing Service voiced their skepticism about the results earned by Escalante's students. The ETS investigates the class for cheating. Ultimately, the service provider had to admit that Escalante's students had honorably achieved their scores. This great teacher challenged their minds and instilled a belief in themselves.

In order for us to get people to feel important, we must see their value. What we look for in people, we can see. What we see, we communicate. What we communicate stimulates people to respond accordingly. What do you see in and expect of others?

REDUCING THE STING
OF CRITICISM

Face it, some people have photographic memories. They remember all the negatives about the people around them. You have probably encountered such a person somewhere in your life and have scrambled to avoid his or her crushing blows. Although it's true that criticism won't kill you, its sting can have a lasting impact.

It's difficult to live out the wisdom of Charles Spurgeon, who said, "Insults are like bad coins; we cannot help their being offered to us, but we need not take them." Easier said than done. Criticism seems to immediately cut its way to our emotional center and leave undesirable scars.

We do have a choice in how we deal with the insults we encounter, and we must realize that no matter how small or large the issue might be, it can be made worse or better by our reaction. When I am criticized, I have a tendency to overreact and become defensive. I dwell on the comment, running it through my mind over and over attempting to justify my actions or prove mentally how wrong the other

A successful man is one who can lay a firm foundation with the bricks that others throw at him.

DAVID
BRINKLEY

person was. Incredible energy is wasted in this spiraling, unproductive activity.

The next time you find yourself in the path of critical bricks hurled your way, learn to desensitize the impact of accusations rather than stand defenseless.

1. Consider the Source. Normally it is the person who can't dance who complains about the unevenness of the floor. Likewise, people who criticize other people are frequently hurting themselves. Out of their frustration with life, they find someone else to blame. Don't take their criticism personally.

While driving along a desolate highway on a hot summer afternoon, I noticed vultures soaring high overhead, swooping down, then rising up again. Their motives were undoubtedly selfish as I watched a small group of them tear apart and devour the remains of a small animal on the side of the road. That's their lifestyle—continually on the lookout for some creature they can take advantage of. Much like the vultures, critical people tend to look for unsuspecting, vulnerable victims they can tear apart and devour. Consider the source before deciding to take seriously what has been said.

2. Smile. Have you ever tried arguing with someone who is smiling at you? If you want to disarm an attacker, take a deep breath, smile, and say, "Thank you." O. A. Bautista says, "One of the surest marks of good character is a person's ability to accept criticism without malice to the one who gives it." I might add that it takes an equally strong character to neutralize criticism before it damages yourself or the relationship. I'm not suggesting that this is easy, but you will find it helpful in keeping critical comments in perspective.

Along with your smile, keep your sense of humor intact. Humor is a marvelous tool for neutralizing the sting of criticism and disapproval. It will divert your attention and diminish the effects.

I love the story of the lady who took her overworked husband to the family physician for a checkup. The physician took the wife aside and whispered: "I don't like the way your husband looks."

"I don't either," she replied, "but he's always been a good provider."

3. Expect It but Don't Accept It. Epictetus provided us an ideal approach to dealing with all those people with photographic memories. "If someone criticizes you, agree at once. Mention that if only the other person knew you well, there would be more to criticize than that." Arguing with one who criticizes is a no-win battle, so Epictetus believed the best way to silence your critics and not waste energy is to agree with them and get on with life.

Someone once said that there are only two critical people in the whole world . . . they just move around a lot and seem to pull down the masses with their criticism. "Nothing takes a greater toll on us than to be around a pessimist—a person always finding fault and criticizing others," said Cavett Robert. "We've all seen the type. He has mental B.O. He's a one-man grievance committee, always in session." Actually, criticism has become a national pastime and sooner or later you will be the target of someone's mental B.O. Not everything everybody says about you is true. It is important that you immediately and objectively weigh the value of the other's comment. Learn what you can from the criticism. If the person is right, make changes. If he or she is wrong, don't spend another moment focused on the accusations.

4. Don't Take It Personally. Abraham Lincoln would never have achieved all he did had he not learned to duck or build on the massive criticism he encountered. His insight is worth your consideration: "If I were to try to read, much less to answer, all the attacks made on me, this shop might as well be closed for any other business," Lincoln said. "I do the very best I know how—the very best I can; and I mean to keep doing so until the end. If the end brings me out all right, then what is said against me won't matter. If the end brings me out wrong, then ten angels swearing I was right would make no difference."

Colonel George Washington Goethals faced enormous opposition as the supervisor responsible for building the Panama Canal. Not only did his builders face incredible challenges with geography, climate, and disease, but people back home predicted they would never complete the "impossible task." The great engineer kept the faith and was resolute in steadily moving forward to complete the project without responding to his opposition.

At one point a frustrated coworker asked, "Aren't you going to answer your critics?" "In time," Goethals replied. "How?" the man asked. The colonel smiled and said, "With the canal!" That answer materialized on August 15, 1914, when the canal opened to traffic for the first time.

Pressing forward. Not getting caught up in verbal warfare. Producing results. Those are often the best ways to counteract ridicule. Expect it. Don't accept it. Press on.

5. Ponder the Benefits. When the legendary Knute Rockne was head football coach at Notre Dame, a column appeared in the school paper with no indication as to who wrote it, other than the signature "Old Bearskin." The columnist picked apart each player, pointing out his individual weaknesses and lambasting his shortcomings and inept performance.

Word spread quickly across campus, and players complained to Rockne that they were being unfairly criticized. Rockne would empathize with their position and encourage them to get out on the field and prove their critic wrong.

The writer of that column was never identified—that is, until after Rockne died. And guess what? "Old Bearskin" was actually the players' best friend and their coach. Yes, Rockne penned the article. He was aware of what happened to football legends whose success on the field went to their heads. As "Old Bearskin," his criticisms were an attempt to help them avoid the pitfalls of pride and strive continually to achieve new levels of performance.

As unfair as criticism might be, it can also be a helpful guardian against the snares of success. Corrie ten Boom believes, "Our critics are the unpaid guardians of our souls." That may be a bit difficult to swallow, but with an open mind the perceptions of others can actually assist us in keeping our talents fine-tuned. The master retailer Marshall Field maintained a healthy attitude about criticism. He said, "Those who enter to buy, support me. Those who come to flatter, please me. Those who complain, teach me how I may please others so that more will come. Only those hurt me who are displeased but do not complain. They refuse me permission to correct my errors and thus improve my service."

I had the unfortunate experience of going to the doctor to determine the source of severe stomach pain. As I lay on the examination table he began to poke, prod, and push in various areas, all the while asking, "Does this hurt? How about this?" It was an unpleasant experience.

When I flinched with pain each time he pressed a certain area, it was evident that he was either pressing too hard, without the right sensitivity, or it was a problem area. In my case, additional tests were required resulting in the diagnosis of an infection and the need for treatment.

So it is with criticism. When you cry out with discomfort, that might be an indication there is need for additional attention. Maybe someone is just pushing a hot button and is not so sensitive as he or she should be. You can't control the critical people in your life. But what you do with criticism is your decision. And you can control the way in which you dish out criticism. Do you do it with kindness and use it to encourage others, or do you wield it as a weapon of destruction? The next time you have criticism of another that you feel you should give, be sure that the ultimate message is one of encouragement.

I can please only one person per day. Today is not your day. Tomorrow isn't looking good either.

DILBERT'S WORDS OF WISDOM

COMMUNICATION

*The reason you don't understand me is
because I'm talkin' to you in English
and you're listenin' in dingbat.*

ARCHIE BUNKER

FOR MEN ONLY

D r. Paul Faulkner believes there is a distinct difference in the listening ability between men and women. In his book *Making Things Right*, Dr. Faulkner suggests that women are wired for 440 volts! They have little emotional wires sticking out from them in all directions. They are wired for sound and two-way communication. They talk and receive. They hook into another person's emotions and needs.

On the other hand, men are wired for 12 volts. That's all. We have two little wires sticking out, and they're both bent. Our speakers are usually hooked up, but our receivers are dead. So we have to work a lot harder to listen than the women do. We're just wired differently. We men are like two tin cans and a waxed string. But the women are hooked up like Ma Bell.

Archie and Edith Bunker's communication difficulties probably had little to do with one speaking English and other

Before a marriage, a man will lie awake all night thinking about something you said; after marriage, he'll fall asleep before you finish saying it.

HELEN
ROWLAND

communicating in "dingbat." Dr. Faulkner might suggest that Archie Bunker give some serious attention to his bent wires and dead receiver.

Now that I think about it, I'm going to put additional effort into my own 12-volt wiring system to improve my reception. What about you?

A GIVING
SPIRIT

Henry Ford suggested, "If there is any one secret to success it lies in the ability to get the other person's point of view and see things from his angle as well as your own." Effective listening plays a major role in our ability to understand situations from another person's perspective, thereby ensuring a mutual understanding. Henry Ford considered this ability so important that he promoted it as a secret to success. Consider these four major principles for successful listening. These practical and proven techniques will increase your impact on people dramatically.

You ain't learnin' nothin' when you're talkin.'
LYNDON B. JOHNSON

1. Develop a Willingness to Listen. Your heart, not your ears, determines your listening efficiency. It has been said that "when the heart is willing it will find a thousand ways, but when the heart is weak it will find a thousand excuses."

A man approached his farmer neighbor one day asking to borrow his rope. "Can't do it," the farmer replied, "I'm using it to tie up my milk."

"You can't tie up your milk with a rope," the borrower responded.

"I know," the farmer replied, "but when you don't want to do something, one excuse is as good as another."

How true! Listening is a desire, an attitude that wants to hear what others are saying. Dick Cavett explained why this attitude is so important. He said, "It's a rare person who wants to hear what he doesn't want to hear." Developing an attitude or wanting to hear is an inside job. You can read all the books, take an array of classes, or indulge yourself with other learning sources but the prerequisite to becoming an effective leader is developing a willingness to listen.

2. Be Open-Minded. "Real communication," wrote Carl Rogers, "takes place when we listen with understanding; that is, see the speaker's idea from his or her viewpoint, sense how they feel about it, and realize why they're talking about it." People can be distracted from achieving this level of communication when they jump to conclusions, find fault with the message, react to emotionally charged words, or allow their prejudices to interfere with what is being said.

I rarely travel in my car without the entertainment of a motivational or educational cassette message playing. Rarely do I argue, interrupt, or yell at my cassette player. Instead, I carefully listen to the speaker's entire message, take a few written notes, and then reflect on what has been said. In other words, even though I might not agree with everything I hear, it is not an option to listen selectively, pay attention only to what I agree with, or block out topics that fail to be appealing. It's critical to hear the whole message without making assumptions that block our ability to understand the other person's perspective.

The word "communication" comes from the Latin root which means "to have in common." When you listen, be open-minded enough to look for common ground. This open-minded approach to listening will increase your comprehension and ability to understand the ideas and feelings being shared.

I fear that far too often our listening minds are like the seasoned consultant. An aspiring management consultant was learning the ropes from an experienced senior partner. As the novice shadowed his model, he noticed how several times a day people would dump their problems on the other man. The experienced consultant would maintain eye contact, nod, and smile warmly. Then it was on to another department where the same scenario would be repeated. Day in and day out the seasoned consultant seemed to patiently listen to everyone's moans and groans.

Finally, the young man could restrain himself no longer. "I don't see how you can do it. How do you put up with listening to everyone's problems all of the time and still remain so positive?"

The older consultant flashed a wry smile and said, "Who listens?"

3. Be Attentive. President Abraham Lincoln said, "When I'm getting ready to reason with a man, I spend one third of my time thinking about myself and what I am going to say—and two thirds thinking about him and what he is going to say." Lincoln, the master communicator, knew how important it was to be attentive to those he was communicating with.

Attentive listening is difficult partly because the normal person can listen at 400–600 words per minute, while the average speaking rate is 200–300 words per minute. That leaves a substantial amount of time for the mind to wander.

Maybe this explains why the normal listener retains only 50 percent of what he or she hears; after 48 hours, retains only 25 percent; and after one week, 10 percent.

In addition, we listen at about a 25 percent efficiency rate. That means that we ignore, misunderstand, or distort a majority of what we hear.

So, how can we increase our attention quotient? Become a sponge. Soak in everything the other person is saying. Soak it up. Everything. Shut out all distractions. Remember, your mind is working at 400–600 words a minute. Therefore, to give someone your undivided attention and soak up the entire message:

Maintain comfortable eye contact. Don't stare.

Don't jump to conclusions and guess what the person is going to say next.

Refrain from interrupting. Let the person finish.

Be patient.

Listen for the spoken and unspoken message.

Don't tune people out. Keep an open mind.

Be silent. Juggle the letters in listen and "silent" emerges.

Take a few notes.

Wait to prepare your reply until the person has finished.

Nod, smile, agree with what is being said, lean slightly forward. Actively participate in the conversation.

Ask questions to clarify.

Don't allow how people say something to distract you from what they say.

Paraphrase what's been said. Make sure you have an accurate picture of the message.

These strategies take tremendous discipline and self-control. You can do it. Commit yourself and avoid the temptation to be distracted. You will pay people the utmost compliment by giving them your undivided attention.

4. Make People Glad That They Talk to You. So often I assume people talk to me because they are looking for advice. More often than not, advice is the last thing they seek. People want a sympathetic ear, one that will sincerely attempt to experience what they are feeling and accept them for it. "After 36 years," said Ann Landers, "I realize that many people who write to me don't want advice. They just need someone who will listen."

A particularly heart-warming story concerning the value of listening involves a young woman asked out on two dates. The first night she went to dinner with William E. Gladstone, the distinguished British diplomat. Upon arriving home, she was asked her opinion of the evening. "Oh," she responded, "William Gladstone is the cleverest man in England."

When her evening with the equally distinguished Benjamin Disraeli was over, the same question was posed to her. She replied thoughtfully, "Benjamin Disraeli made me feel like the cleverest woman in England."

What was the difference? It has been said that listening to someone is the highest form of compliment you can pay. That person will feel valued by your attention to them and what they have to say. Disraeli was known for his listening skills and it only followed that an evening spent with him would make anyone feel important.

George and Nikki Kochler mirror the importance of affirming people through listening: "When you and I listen to another person we are conveying the thought that 'I'm interested in you as a person, and I think that what you feel is important. I respect your thoughts, even if I don't agree with them. I know that they are valid for you. I feel sure that you have a contribution to make. I'm not trying to change you or evaluate you. I just want to understand you. I think you're worth listening to, and I want you to know that I'm the kind of person that you can talk to.'"

Is that the attitude that permeates your conversations? A credible way to evaluate that question is to answer this one: How important do people feel after spending time with me?

One often reads about the art of conversation—how it's dying or what's needed to make it flourish, or how rare good ones are. But wouldn't you agree that the infinitely more valuable rara avis *is a good listener?*

MALCOLM FORBES

UNTANGLE YOUR HORNS

For some of the large indignities of life, the best remedy is direct action. For the small indignities, the best remedy is a Charlie Chaplin movie. The hard part is knowing the difference.

CAROL
TAVRIS

I am told that displayed in an old monastery near Babenhausen, Germany are two pairs of deer antlers permanently interlocked. Apparently they were found in that position many years ago. Legend has it the animals had been fighting fiercely, and their horns became so entangled they were unable to free themselves. As a result, both deer perished from hunger.

Imagine those entangled horns. They represent the frozen condition conflict can create. When we are determined to have our own way, win every argument, or demand our rights, we risk becoming entangled to the degree that we starve a relationship. Unresolved conflict threatens to dissolve relationships.

Heightened negative emotions can also spread to those outside the initial conflict. That's what happened in the spring of 1894 when the Baltimore Orioles arrived in Boston to play a regular season, a routine baseball game. The game became anything but routine when a clash occurred between two players.

The Orioles' John McGraw got into a fight with the Boston third baseman. Within minutes both benches emptied to join the brawl. People in the grandstands decided to get involved and the conflict between fans erupted. Someone set fire to the stands, and eventually the entire ballpark burned to the ground. To make matters worse, the fire spread to 107 other Boston buildings. This unnecessary conflict turned into a community disaster.

Conflicts are inevitable, but such devastating effects can be avoided. We bring different backgrounds, experiences, opinions, and emotions into our relationships. Whenever two people interact on an ongoing basis there is bound to be some discord. Having conflict need not be perceived as abnormal. The real issue is whether or not we get it resolved.

Past experiences certainly affect our present approaches to conflict. When I was growing up my two brothers and I would periodically get into a wing-ding of an argument. My mother would immediately intercede, separate us, and tell us each to go to our rooms until we could learn to get along. But think about that a minute. It is impossible to learn how to get along with people when you are separated from them. At any rate, when I encounter conflict today, my first reaction is to go to my room (or someplace else where I can be alone).

Unfortunately, when I come out of my room the conflict is still waiting for me.

There's no magic solution for resolving conflict. There are, however, a number of actions we can take to diffuse tense situations and move toward resolving the issues.

1. Strive for Mutual Benefit. The ridiculousness of selfish, unsettled disputes was exhibited by a man in Cresco, Iowa a few years ago. He made a half-car garage out of a one-car garage by hiring a contractor to saw the structure in half. The sawing was the climax to a property-line dispute between Halsted and the owner of a small adjoining lot. When it was learned that Halsted's garage straddled the line between the two properties, negotiations over his use of the garage broke down, and he had the half not on his property cut down.

There is no use pursuing resolution to any conflict unless you are willing to seek an agreement that is mutually beneficial. It's imperative for people to focus on what's right for people, not who's right. I learned a long time ago that supposed winners in a conflict don't learn anything and losers never forget who stepped on them to get their way.

2. Seek Understanding. I am working on an invention that will revolutionize the world of negotiations. Once perfected, I predict this invention will eliminate conflict.

What is it? An Ego Enema. Countless relationship struggles would be solved if we could eliminate egos from the formula.

"If you don't agree with me," Sam Markewich said, "it means you haven't been listening." His comment would indicate that there are basically two sides to any argument—our side and the side that no intelligent, informed, breathing, sane, or self-respecting person could possibly hold. See what I mean about needing an Ego Enema?

Most people think they see the world as it is, but they don't. They see the world as they are. We perceive situations based on who we are, not on other people's perspectives. Try to see the world the way they see it. Be sensitive to others' emotions. Emotions are neither right nor wrong. Accept people and their opinions. Attempt to understand their perspective concerning the issues. Realize their priorities may not be yours, and the reasons behind their convictions could shed valuable light on the entire situation. Maintain calmness and patience as you listen to others talk. Accept your personal differences and move on.

3. Focus on the Problem. Get the facts. Don't rely on assumptions. Any time a conflict occurs, it is wise to make sure both parties are reading the same page. Refrain from attacking people and stay clear of arguing. Avoid fighting, battling, or trying to overcome another's opinions or behavior. Insults, accusations, and blaming are dead-end strategies.

Aristotle had a good point. "How many a dispute could have been deflated into a single paragraph," he said, "if the disputants had dared to define their terms." Resolution isn't possible by dealing with symptoms. Define your terms by first defining the problem. Please make sure you agree on what the REAL problem is.

4. Find a Point of Agreement. You've heard it said that sometimes people just need to learn to agree to disagree. That might be true, but I much prefer a different approach before resigning myself to that conclusion. Cullen Hightower said: "There's too much said for the sake of argument and too little said for the sake of agreement." I like being around agreeable people with whom I can freely and openly discuss issues, concerns, or topics that we don't necessarily agree on. Being agreeable involves the ability to smile, nod, and express respect for another person's position.

Whenever you are intent on being disagreeable, other people will feel challenged and their intelligence will be questioned. Telling someone they are flat-out wrong will immediately raise the defenses, heighten their stubbornness, and cause them to be more adamant about their position.

How about agreeing to find out what we can agree on and committing our efforts to building on the things we can agree on and moving beyond the disagreements?

There is an old saying that goes, "Agree with thine adversary quickly." Help others be right about as many things as possible and you'll be amazed at how quickly the resistance will subside on other things.

5. Generate Solutions. Don't get stuck dwelling on the problem—just agree on it and then move on to the creatively stimulating process of generating solutions. "You cannot shake hands," said Golda Meir, "with a clenched fist." Neither can you generate solutions to a disagreement with a one-track mind or private agenda. What are ALL of the possible solutions that will produce a mutual benefit?

6. Determine a Win–Win Plan of Action. The motivation behind every conflict discussion should be to reach a point where we can genuinely agree on a solution that benefits each of us. Give way on the minor points of disagreement that have become a thorn in the flesh. Look for major points of agreement that will be mutually beneficial. Find ways to nurture the other person's self-esteem. Be likable, respectful, and considerate rather than being intimidating and demanding—you'll get much further. Try to

There comes a time in the affairs of (people) when you must take the bull by the tail and face the situation.

W. C. FIELDS

❊

love that person on the other end as you accept differences and capitalize on agreements.

Too often people approach arguments like the man who said to his coworker: "OK, I'll meet you halfway. I will admit I'm right if you'll admit you're wrong."

In an issue of *Pulpit Helps* a humorous tale appeared about a hunter who had his gun aimed at a large bear and was ready to pull the trigger. Just then the bear spoke in a soft, soothing voice, saying, "Isn't it better to talk than to shoot? Why don't we negotiate the matter? What is it you want?" The hunter lowered his rifle and answered, "I would like a fur coat." "That's good," said the bear. "I think that's something we can talk about. All I want is a full stomach; maybe we can reach a compromise." So they sat down to talk it over. A little while later the bear walked away alone. The negotiations had been successful—the bear had a full stomach, and the hunter had a fur coat!

This far-fetched fable embodies healthy advice for arriving at win–win solutions (although had I been the hunter I believe I would have spent a bit more time in the generating-solutions stage). A great way to keep our horns unlocked is to start and end any discussion with these questions: "What is it the other person wants? How can both of our needs be met?"

WORK THROUGH IT

A husband and wife who were having problems in their marriage asked their pastor for counsel. After a rather lengthy session with them, he realized that he wasn't making any progress in resolving their conflicts. Noticing a cat and a dog lying side by side in front of the fireplace, he said, "Look at how peaceful they are. They certainly don't see eye to eye on everything." The husband commented, "Yes, but just tie them together and see what happens!"

Marriage is a mutual admiration society in which one person is always right, and the other is always the husband.

MARY MARTIN

"A marriage without conflicts," says Andre Maurois, "is almost as inconceivable as a nation without crises."

Maurois's comment reminded me of a judge in a divorce case who asked the husband, "Can you tell the court what passed between you and your wife during your heated argument that prompted the two of you to seek this separation?"

"I sure can, your honor," the man nervously responded, "there was a toaster, two knives, and a set of crystal."

Although amusing, this incident reminds us that conflict is normal; marital wars are dangerous.

Face it: The unique union of a man and woman is bound to create some issues of incompatibility. The transition from a casual to a formal relationship makes George Levinger's advice especially important. He said, "What counts in making a happy marriage is not so much how compatible you are, but how you deal with incompatibility. Differences that existed before marriage are intensified when we live with them. We come from different backgrounds, possess our own personality, see the world from unique perspectives, and are the unfortunate owners of irritating habits. We don't think alike, respond to life alike, or act alike. It can be frustrating. Rather than allowing the relationship to get tied up in knots, learn to loosen the noose a bit."

Author Charles Swindoll, writing in Commitment: *The Key to Marriage*, discusses the reality of conflict in marriage.

"There is no such thing as a home completely without conflicts. The last couple to live 'happily ever after' was Snow White and Prince Charming. Even though you are committed to your mate, there will still be times of tension, tears, struggle, disagreement, and impatience. Commitment doesn't erase our humanity! That's bad news, but it's realistic."

Although normal, work through conflict. Don't allow your behaviors to elevate it.

Ogden Nash suggested: "To keep your marriage brimming, with love in the loving cup, when you're wrong, admit it. When you're right, shut up."

There will always be a battle between the sexes because men and women want different things. Men want women and women want men.

GEORGE BURNS

A DIFFERENCE
OF OPINION

*In every house
of marriage
there is room
for an
interpreter.*

STANLEY
KUNITZ

❋

Our monthly card club tended to stray from the bridge game we came to play to conversations about local news, our children's activities, and sports events. One Saturday night a discussion ensued about marriage, men's irritating habits (from the women's perspective), and women's misconceptions about men (from the men's viewpoint). It was a lighthearted, give-and-take debate that digressed into a competition to see who could share the most cynical philosophy.

My favorite bantering came from a happily married couple with a great sense of humor.

The husband explained the key to their model marriage: "My wife and I understand each other. I don't try to run her life, and I don't try to run mine."

Not to be outdone, his wife responded, "The real secret to us staying married such a long time is simple, one of us talks, and the other doesn't listen."

AN IRISH PRAYER

May those who love us, love us;
And those who don't love us,
May God turn their hearts,
And if He doesn't turn their hearts,
May He turn their ankles,
So we'll know them by their limping.

GRATITUDE

*Husbands, take your wife on at least one date
a week. It doesn't have to be expensive
(or fancy) but one that calls for dressing up
a little for each other and providing
undisturbed time together.*

RALPH L. BYRON

KEEP THOSE FIRES BURNING

It's no secret that romantic gratification or the lack of it are factors in every marriage. The idea of having one date together a week is a great way to keep the romantic fires burning. Undisturbed private time allows you to be continually reacquainted and in tune with each other's needs.

The following story provides a humorous look at one person's experience:

Mr. Smith came home from work early and found his wife in bed with a handsome young man. Just as Mr. Smith was about to storm out, she stopped him and said, "Before you leave, I'd like you to know how this happened.

"When I was driving home from shopping this afternoon, I hit a hole in the pavement. The hole was filled with water. Great blobs of mud spattered all over this man. Without a trace of anger, he looked at me and said, 'What rotten luck. I have a very important meeting this afternoon and just look at me!'

"I told him that I was terribly sorry and offered to clean him up. He seemed grateful, and I brought him home.

"He undressed in the bathroom, and I handed him the bathrobe I bought you for Christmas a few years ago. It no longer closes in front because of your pot belly.

"While his clothes were drying, I gave him lunch—the casserole you missed last night because you decided to go out with the guys after work. He said it was the best home-cooked meal he had had in months. I told him it was the first compliment I had received about my cooking in years.

"We talked while I pressed his shirt, and it was wonderful to have a conversation with a man who seemed interested in what I had to say. Suddenly he noticed the ironing board was wobbly. I had asked you a dozen times to fix it, but you were always too busy. The man fixed the ironing board in ten minutes, and then he actually put the tools away.

"As he was about to leave, he asked with a smile, 'Is there anything else your husband has neglected lately?' And that is the end of my story!"

James C. Dobson equals this story with one of his own. Dobson claims he knows an obstetrician who is deaf and blind in the same way. It seems the obstetrician called a physician friend of Dobson's, asking for a favor.

"My wife has been having some abdominal problems and she's in particular discomfort this afternoon," he said. "I don't want to treat my own wife and wonder if you'd see her for me?"

The physician invited the doctor to bring his wife for an examination, whereupon he discovered (are you ready for this?) that she was five months pregnant! Her obstetrician husband was so busy caring for other patients that he hadn't even noticed his wife's burgeoning pregnancy. "I must admit wondering," comments Dobson, "how in the world this woman ever got his attention long enough to conceive!"

James Smith wrote, "The tragedy of western marriages is that most of us quit courting once we're married."

Have you been taking your spouse for granted? What are you waiting for? Set the time now for your next date, and plan something unexpected to show your spouse that he or she is truly valued in your life.

The difference between courtship and marriage is the difference between the pictures in the seed catalog and what comes up.

AUTHOR UNKNOWN

HERE'S HOW TO PHRASE IT WHEN YOU WANT TO PRAISE IT

In spite of our supersonic generation, high-tech wizardry, and computer gadgetry, there is no technical tool equal to praise.
JERRY D. TWENTIER

❦

Upon accepting an award, Jack Benny once remarked, "I really don't deserve this. But I have arthritis and I don't deserve that either."

Wouldn't it be great if appreciation would become as natural to give as undesirable life experiences were to contract? Yet how many times do small, seemingly insignificant actions go unnoticed? The doers of such tasks feel they would be better off getting attention in unacceptable ways.

Consider the employee who comes in late one morning only to be greeted by his supervisor who says, "Sam, you're late!"

Sam goes about his duties thinking, "So that's what I need to do to get noticed. Day in and day out I do my job without anyone paying any attention. Come in late and, finally, they know I'm working here."

People want to believe their efforts deserve praise, and they are willing to go to great lengths to receive it. Yet, expressing appreciation is one of the most neglected acts in relationships. When you observe people doing good things, let them know you recognized it. How? Glad you asked. Here are some simple phrases that will help you praise people and encourage them to repeat their positive behavior:

"I appreciate the way you . . ."

"I'm impressed with . . ."

"You're terrific because . . ."

"Thanks for going all out when you . . ."

"One of the things I enjoy most about you is . . ."

"I admire your . . ."

"Great job with . . ."

"I really enjoy working with you because . . ."

"Our team couldn't be successful without your . . ."

"Thank you for your . . ."

"You made my day when . . ."

"You can be proud of your . . ."

"You did an outstanding job of . . ."

"It's evident you have the ability to . . ."

"I like your . . ."

"You deserve a pat on the back for . . ."

"You should be proud of yourself for . . ."

"I admire the way you take the time to . . ."

"You're really good at . . ."

"You've got my support with . . ."

"What a great idea!"

"It's evident you have a special knack of . . ."

"You were a great help when . . ."

"You have a special gift for . . ."

"I enjoy being with you because you . . ."

"You're doing a top-notch job of . . ."

"It's fun watching you . . ."

"I know you can do it!"

"I believe in you."

"Your commitment to _____ is appreciated!"

The power of positive praise is limited only by its lack of use. How many people do you know who could benefit from a sincere "congratulations" or "great job" or possibly even "you're the best"? Silent appreciation doesn't mean much. Let others know you value them. They'll live up to your expectations.

Samuel Goldwyn said, "When someone does something good, applaud! You will make two people happy." I've provided a sampling of phrases you can use to applaud people. Use them frequently. Find additional ways to praise and increase people's good feelings about themselves. You'll be happy you did.

I believe that you should praise people whenever you can; it causes them to respond as a thirsty plant responds to water.

MARY KAY ASH

VALUE YOUR FRIENDS

Friendship is a strong habitual inclination in two persons to promote the good and happiness of one another.

EUSTACE
BUDGELL

Socrates once asked an elderly man what he was most thankful for. The man replied, "That being such as I am, I have had the friends I have had."

When we count up the truly valuable treasures of life, friendships certainly ought to be toward the top of the list. As all other tangible life rewards drift away, our friendships warrant whatever energy it takes to keep them alive and healthy. Consider the wisdom offered throughout history on ways to maintain, value, and enrich our friendships.

Friendship is built upon the commitment to be a friend, not upon the desire to have a friend.

AUTHOR UNKNOWN

If the people around you don't believe in you, if they don't encourage you, then you need to find some people who do.

JOHN MAXWELL

Do not use a hatchet to remove a fly from your friend's forehead.

CHINESE PROVERB

Any one who has had a long life of experience is worth listening to, worth emulating, and worth trying to have as a friend.

GEORGE MATTHEW ADAMS

The proper office of a friend is to side with you when you are in the wrong. Nearly anybody will side with you when you are right.

MARK TWAIN

A loyal friend laughs at your jokes when they're not so good, and sympathizes with your problems when they are not so bad.

ARNOLD H. GLASOW

The glory of friendship is not in the outstretched hand, nor the kindly smile, nor the joy of companionship; it is in the spiritual inspiration that comes to one when he discovers that someone else believes in him and is willing to trust him.

RALPH WALDO EMERSON

A true friend is one who hears and understands when you share your deepest feelings. He supports you when you are struggling; he corrects you, gently and with love, when you err; and he forgives you when you fail. A true friend prods you to personal growth, stretches you to your full potential. And most amazing of all, he celebrates your successes as if they were his own.

RICHARD EXLEY

Be careful the environment you choose for it will shape you; be careful the friends you choose for you will become like them.

W. CLEMENT STONE

Friend: One who knows all about you and loves you just the same.

ELBERT HUBBARD

You can always tell a real friend. When you've made a fool of yourself, he doesn't feel you've done a permanent job.

AUTHOR UNKNOWN

PART II

THE SIMPLE SECRETS *of* HAPPINESS AT WORK

INFUSE YOUR
WORK WITH
PASSION

*Motivation is a fire from within. If someone
else tries to light that fire under you,
chances are it will burn briefly.*

STEPHEN COVEY

LIGHT YOURSELF
ON FIRE

"Once upon a time there was a guy named Joe who had a very lousy job." Those are the opening words of Stephen Spielberg's 1990 movie, *Joe Versus the Volcano*.

In the movie, Joe Banks (Tom Hanks) reaches a point of total frustration with his job and his life. Everyday is bad Monday. His boss is always in a bad mood. The cumulative stresses convince Joe his energy-stripped life is irreparable. Exasperated and depressed, he laments, "I'm losing my soul." Soon after Joe learns he is plagued with terminal "brain cloud" (a fictitious diagnosis that convinced Joe he was mentally asleep).

Unemployed and desperate, Joe coincidentally encounters an eccentric jillionaire (played by Lloyd Bridges) who presents a proposition that allows Joe to turn his mediocre, dead-end, unfulfilled life around. All he must do in return is

Success is not the result of spontaneous combustion. You must set yourself on fire.

REGGIE LEACH

journey to the island of Waponi Woo and leap into a volcano. Joe leaps at the chance.

Aboard the jillionaire's yacht, Joe meets Patricia, one of the wealthy man's daughters. In awe of the incredible turn of events and the new life he has enjoyed since meeting her father, Joe looks into the moonless, star-filled night and exclaims, "Your life is unbelievable—just unbelieveable!"

Patricia's response was profound. "My father says that almost the whole world is asleep—everybody you know, everybody you see, everybody you talk to. He says that only a few people are awake, and they live in a state of constant, total amazement."

The movie was a commercial disaster and a popular target of cynical movie critics who missed this scene, or at least misinterpreted Spielberg's attempt at jolting people into "waking up."

Paul Goodman, the famous linguist and social commentator, estimated that as many as 82 percent of American workers don't like being at work and can't wait to be freed from what work does to them. They are the Joe Bankses of the world who need an immediate wake-up call, preferably (for them) without the threat of terminal "brain cloud."

People who depend on others for the condition of their morale do themselves a huge disservice. No organization or supervisor can adequately be empowered to pump you up.

It's so popular today to plead victimization by the system, circumstances, competition, rightsizing, or other external factor. Human spirits are buffeted by increased pressures from co-workers, job demands, or the daily grind of everyday living. Indifference slithers in to replace motivation and a vicious cycle of unhappiness begins.

Blaming, finger-pointing, and accusing are popular anecdotes for attitudes gone sour. Steer free from such self-defeating behavior. Take charge of your moods. Fill your energy tank. Corral negative emotions. Bury grudges and perceived unfairness. Recognize your present mental attitudes about the job and get serious about an action plan to help you out of the ruts.

There is an old Texas saying that indicates "You can't light a fire with a wet match." What's your "flammable quotient"? Are your coals smoldering? Are the flames hot and high?

Are you alive with excitement about your work? Are you doing what you love? Light yourself on fire. Become a passionate, self-igniting morale arsonist rather than operating on the erroneous assumption that someone else will make your job more exciting or more challenging.

I often ask applicants what prompted them to apply at our organization. It never ceases to amaze me how many people respond, "I thought you might have a job I would like." Sorry. We don't have any jobs like that. However, we do have a lot of people who like their jobs.

Your job (no matter how great or lousy it is) can be more than a way to earn a living. Make it an important element in creating a quality life. You don't need to jump into a volcano to light yourself on fire. Reenergizing your work spirit is an inside job.

THE MONEY
IS THE GRAVY

Denis Waitley, in *Empires of the Mind,* shared the experience of attending his daughter's college graduation. Fearing the exercises would be long and merciless, Waitley was relieved when the keynote speaker took the podium. The speaker was Edward James Olmos, the actor–activist who played Jaime Escalante in an inspiring movie about inner-city students called *Stand and Deliver.*

According to Waitley, Olmos stood up, removed his cap, and regarded the graduates. "So we're ready to party?" he asked. "Yeah, let's party!" they answered in unison. "I know, thank God it's Friday," he resumed. "But commencement means to begin, not finish. You've had a four-year sabbatical from life, and now you're ready to go out there and earn. You're only beginning Real World 101 in your education.

"One more thing before we leave," he continued. "Please never, ever work for money. Please don't just get a job. A job is something that many of you had while you were working

To fulfill a dream, to be allowed to sweat over lonely labor, to be given a chance to create, is the meat and potatoes of life. The money is the gravy.

The Lonely Life

your way through college. A job is something you do for money. But a career is something you do because you must do it. You want to do it, you love doing it, you're excited when you do it. And you'd do it even if you were paid nothing beyond food and basics. You do it because it's your life."

Rarely does our educational training prepare us to find a career that is satisfying. We go to college, learn skills, and then find a company that offers a paycheck in exchange for our knowledge and a few hours of work. If only we could inject every college graduate and potential employee with this admonishment, "Pursue a passion, not a paycheck." This simple insight could save a multitude of people from being disillusioned. Charles Schwab, steel magnate, concluded: "The man who does not work for the love of work but only for money is not likely to make money nor find much fun in life." No matter how little or how much your chosen career pays in money, if you pursue it with passion, you'll go to work every day with the satisfaction of knowing you are making a difference.

We all need the money. That is a given. But, work goes beyond what you do to earn a paycheck; it involves personal commitment, personal satisfaction, and personal growth. Like it or not, these results—along with promotions and pay increases—are rewards for achieving results, not just doing work. Results are realized when we apply and develop our strengths. In *Goodbye Job, Hello Me,* Wexler and Wolf suggest, "The fascination of simply making money wears thin in time. The real fruits of one's labors are seen in the planting of one's gifts." When you are involved in a company that shares your values and you are doing a job that utilizes your talents and skills, a meaningful career will blossom.

"Is my occupation what I get paid money for, or is it something larger and wider and richer—more a matter of what I am or how I think about myself," questioned Robert Fulghum. "Making a living and having a life are not the same thing. Making a living and making a life that's worthwhile are not the same thing. A job title doesn't even come close to answering the question, 'What do you do?' Possessing a title or allowing money to possess you does not answer the questions, "Who are you?" or "What do you do?"

People want jobs that matter. Tom Brokaw said, "It's easy to make a buck. It's a lot tougher to make a difference." What makes this difficult is that each of us must discover for ourselves what activities are meaningful and allow us the opportunity to make a difference. If you've been feeling disenfranchised, unmotivated, dissatisfied, or apathetic,

First find something you like to do so much you'd gladly do it for nothing; then learn to do it so well people are happy to pay you for it.

WALT DISNEY

there's a chance you've not yet realized that it takes more than money to light the fire of passion.

How many people do you know work in a job they dislike so they can earn enough money to do the things they like to do? What a dead-end, dissatisfying, unfulfilling way to approach a job.

Historically, people have viewed work as a required necessity to make a living, but actually living was reserved for after-hours. Times are changing. There's a visible epidemic among people questioning what they really want out of life and work. A paycheck and a few benefits are no longer sufficient to generate passion and achieve meaning.

Immerse yourself in whatever you are doing. Don't go to work because you have to. Go to work to make a difference. Instead of complaining that you can't find a job you like, concentrate on what you like about your job. Transform your thinking and design strategies to creatively enhance the contribution you make. View yourself as a little company inside of the larger one. Hold yourself accountable for the success of your department. You are the organization. What you do matters. And, remember "The money is the gravy."

CONTENTMENT BREEDS
DISCONTENTMENT

It's dangerous to rest on our past successes. In the book *The Eighty-Yard Run,* a college freshman at his first football practice breaks loose for an 80-yard touchdown run. His teammates immediately place him in high esteem and the coach lets him know he will have quite a future with the team. His pretty blonde girlfriend picks him up after practice and awards him with a passionate kiss. He has the feeling his life is now set, his future secure.

If I see myself today as I was in the past, my past must resurrect itself and become my future.
WILLIAM JAMES

Unfortunately, nothing in his life ever matches that day again. His football experiences never rise above the level of mediocrity, nor does his business career. His marriage goes sour and the disappointment is even greater because he continually reflects back on that day of glory when he was convinced that life would always be pleasant and act favorably toward him.

This young man, and the rest of humankind for that matter, could learn something from the Wisconsin dairy industry. On the side of their milk bottles are printed these words: "Our cows are not contented. They're anxious to do better."

Contentment breeds discontentment. When you're satisfied with savoring the past, in lieu of creating your future, the present loses its appeal. Aspiring to excel, our last achievement inspires us to grow beyond the present. Continuing to think about the same things day after day or attempting to build our lives based on the past is anti-productive. Don't get me wrong, your past is important, but only to the degree your experiences inspire you to new levels of living. Life is more meaningful when you are searching for ways to exceed your past performance, not being content with it.

Johann Wolfgang von Goethe hit a nerve when he said, "Things that matter most must never be at the mercy of things that matter least." Contentment with your favorite foods, road to work, most watched television programs, most frequently worn outfit, and the like is just fine—although I would suggest a little variation to put some spice in your life. These are trivial issues compared to the performance practices, habits, attitudes, approach to problems, relation-ship skills, and other "most" items Goethe alluded to, that significantly affect your future success.

Many years ago, an aspiring Greek artist named Timanthes submitted himself to the instruction of a well-known tutor. Working diligently for several years, the young artist created a portrait that displayed the artistic talent he had developed. Thrilled with the outcome, Timanthes sat day after day gazing at his work.

Early one morning he arrived at the studio to discover his teacher had destroyed his masterpiece. Devastated, angry, and drowning in his tears, he begged an explanation from his tutor. The wise artist replied, "I did it for your own good. That painting was retarding your progress. It was an excellent piece of art, but it was not perfect. Start again and see if you can do even better."

Stunned, yet stimulated, Timanthes put his brush to the canvas and eventually produced a masterpiece called "Sacrifice of Iphigenia."

Fight hard to remain free of long-term contentment and satisfaction with your past accomplishments. Strive for higher plateaus. You'll never have to look back and wish you could go there. It's exciting to work and live with positive anticipation for what can happen next. As Disney's Pocahantas said, "You'll see things you never knew you never knew."

Workers develop routines when they do the same job for a while. They lose their edge, falling into habits not just in what they do but in how they think. Habits turn into routines. Routines into ruts.

ROBERT KRIEGEL

THERE'S NO NEED
TO BE MISERABLE

When I'm
happy I feel
like crying, but
when I'm sad
I don't feel
like laughing.
I think it's
better to be
happy. Then
you get two
feelings for the
price of one.
LILY TOMLIN
AS "EDITH
ANN"

❀

How happy are you with your job? Are there times when misery is more prevalent than happiness? Have you learned to be happy in spite of circumstances, job responsibilities, or people?

Norman Cousins, the late author and editor of *Saturday Review,* wrote, "Happiness is probably the easiest emotion to feel, the most elusive to create deliberately, and the most difficult to define. It is experienced differently by different people." Although happiness is different for each of us, here are a few generic principles worth thinking about.

1. End the search. People who place the search for happiness as the top priority in their life will struggle to experience it. "Happiness is a butterfly—the more you chase it, the more it flies away from you and hides," wrote Rabbi Harold Kushner in the best-selling book *When All You've Ever Wanted Isn't Enough.* "But stop chasing it, put away your net and busy yourself with other, more productive things than the pursuit of happiness, and it will sneak up on you from behind and perch on your shoulder."

2. Evaluate your expectations. Thinking you can be happy with your job all the time is an unrealistic expectation. It won't happen, no matter how hard you try, even if you read every word in this book and implement each suggestion. When you expect your job to make you happy, you've already put yourself in a disadvantageous position. Add to this a desperate pursuit of this elusive emotion and you'll understand why so many people are miserable in their job.

For the most part, I expect to enjoy a happy, satisfied, fulfilled career. But when it doesn't happen, a sense of misery and discontent settles in. Within moments, I'm acutely aware of how my expectations and reality are in conflict. It's a natural setup for disappointment. Author Max Lucado offers this valuable advice, "Remember, disappointment is caused by unmet expectations. Disappointment is cured by revamped expectations." It's a huge mistake to set our expectations so high that they are unattainable or depend on our work to be the sole source of happiness. The problem, of course, is that only rarely do our jobs, other people, or life in general live up to the expected ideal.

3. Exit your misery. Actor and singer Dean Martin died a few years ago. His closest friends commented upon his death that, although he had now died physically, Dean Martin had given up on life years earlier. After his son died in a plane crash, Martin was vocal about his loss of interest in living. Without his son, he no longer wanted to live himself and yearned to die. Friends tried to help him through these difficult times, but Martin was intent that life was over for him. He became a recluse, refused to see friends, and spent his days watching television by himself. His son's tragic death overwhelmed his desire to live.

It's a dangerous thing to hang our happiness on the shoulders of some other person, a career, or a business. As tragic as the event was, Dean Martin still had a lot of life to live. He could have toured with his good friend Frank Sinatra, relished the offers of dinner and enjoyed fellowship with close friends, or poured himself into a number of useful causes. Instead, he gave up on life. He is not alone in this response.

I certainly am not implying that our work compares in value to our relationships. Yet, when people die, life does go on. We grieve. We reflect. We cherish the good times. Expectations are adjusted. We go on. Likewise, we will experience disappointment, unmet expectations, and the death of dreams and goals in our work lives. We refocus, carefully monitoring our reactions, and push forward. It is simply a waste of time and talent to give up and give in to misery.

4. Entertain an agenda other than your own.

I received an article from an unknown source titled "How to Be Miserable." It says, "Think about yourself. Talk about yourself. Use 'I' as often as possible. Mirror yourself continually in the opinion of others. Listen greedily to what people say about you. Expect to be appreciated. Be suspicious. Be jealous and envious. Be sensitive to slights. Never forgive a criticism. Trust nobody but yourself. Insist on consideration and respect. Demand agreement with your own views on everything. Sulk if people are not grateful to you for favors shown them. Never forget a service you have rendered. Shirk your duties if you can. Do as little as possible for others."

I often find the people most unhappy with their work are those who choose to constantly think about themselves and how unhappy they are. The happiest people I encounter are so busy creating and enjoying life, they don't even think about being happy. Their happiness is a by-product of the unselfish effort they put forth. Greta Palmer wisely observed, "Those only are happy who have their minds on some object other than their own happiness—on the happiness of others, on the improvement of mankind, even on some art or pursuit followed not as a means but as itself an ideal end."

5. Expand your thinking. Dale Carnegie suggested that, "Happiness doesn't depend upon who you are or what you have; it depends solely upon what you think." If you continually think about yourself—what you want, the desire for a more exciting job, dissatisfaction with your salary, the need for a vacation, a better boss, or simply for the sun to shine to brighten your spirits—then misery rather than happiness will remain your companion. Remove yourself from the temptation of sponsoring a personal pity party and do something about what you can do something about. Get on with it. You'll be amazed at how quickly your actions will modify your thinking and emotions.

6. Energize the current situation. Being happy in a job that isn't what you thought it would be—or should be—isn't easy. If you fall into the category of the people continually dissatisfied with their jobs, there is hope. You do have a choice to be happier on the job by focusing and acting on the influences within your control. You can also decide to remain forever miserable.

Charlie "Tremendous" Jones reminds us that, "If you can't be happy where you are, it's a cinch you can't be happy where you ain't." In other words, if you can't be happy now with what you have, with what you do and who you are, you will not be happy when you get what you think you want. Happiness comes with learning the skill of living each moment and making the best of it. Certain experiences, job tasks, and people might make it easier for us to be happy, but they do not have the power to make you happy unless you allow them to. You have a choice to be happy or unhappy with your circumstances. Because you are one or the other, why not choose happiness.

When unhappiness reveals its ugly head, remind yourself of the temporary nature of misery—if you choose it to be. Happiness won't resurrect itself if we sulk and brood about the fact that we aren't so happy as we think we should be or would like to be. "It's good to be just plain happy," suggests Henry Miller. "It's a little better to know that you're happy; but to understand that you're happy and to know why and how . . . and still be happy, be happy in the being and the knowing, well that is beyond happiness, that is bliss." Master this attitude and as you move forward in life, you'll notice that happiness follows you. Stop chasing happiness and allow it to catch up with you.

To experience happiness, we must train ourselves to live in this moment, to savor it for what it is, not running ahead in anticipation of some future date nor lagging behind in the paralysis of the past.
LUCI SWINDOLL

GOOD ENOUGH
NEVER IS

Then let us all do what is right, strive with all our might toward the unattainable, develop as fully as we can the gifts God has given us, and never stop learning.

LUDWIG VON BEETHOVEN

LEARNERS WILL INHERIT
THE FUTURE

I t's hard to believe, watching Peter Jennings on the "ABC Evening News," that he wasn't always a smooth anchorperson. His first experience, while in his twenties, did not establish him as an experienced, audience-friendly journalist.

My job is so secret that even I don't know what I'm doing.
WILLIAM
WEBSTER

After three years in his anchor position, Jennings made a bold move. He quit his envious position reading the news and retreated into the trenches to refine his skills as a working reporter. In their informative book, *Anchors: Brokaw, Jennings, Rather and the Evening News,* Robert Goldberg and Gerald Jay Goldberg provide an insightful look at Jennings's journey to becoming a respected TV journalist. They describe how Jennings, who never finished college, used the road as his educational classroom. He covered a wide variety of stories in the United States, became the first network correspondent on permanent assignment in the Middle East, moved to London, and covered other cities in Europe before returning to the anchor slot at ABC.

To be successful in today's business environment, you would be wise to seek hands-on experiences, intellectual stimulation, and an appreciation for information that can boost your effectiveness. Climbing the career ladder or attaining a positive reputation in your current position is precipitated by the ability to learn, absorb, adapt, and apply information that keeps your skills on the cutting edge. You need to be accountable for continually auditing your skill level through self-reflection and pursuing opportunities that take your professionalism to the next level.

By reading, listening, taking risks, and gaining exposure to new experiences, you can overcome ignorance that breeds complacency and blocks career vitality. Professional competence requires a consistent updating of your skill portfolio and the ability to stimulate learning throughout your entire work life. Make your job your classroom. Your knowledge bank is valuable to the organization and keeps your skills from becoming outdated. When your job is flowing smoothly, double your learning. When times are challenging, and the demands are high, quadruple your learning. Learning is a marvelous offense in a radically changing world.

Ironically, a history of professional success can decelerate growth. Satisfaction with the past and present inhibits accelerated learning and adaptability. Without shifting your attitudes to an insatiable quest for creative and expansive learning, you will lose your vitality by resting on the past. A continuum of learning insures the removal of complacency and an increase in competency. No matter how successful you are, without investing in your personal growth, the risk of sinking into repetitious and hypnotic activity is inevitable. The key to sustained success is to keep learning. Probe, adjust, adapt, and develop in new directions.

Look for people who will challenge you. No matter how competent you are, never allow your ego to swell to the point that you shut out the expertise of others. Enlist the help of a friend, a mentor to tell you truthfully where you can grow, expand your talents, or seek new possibilities. You want someone who will challenge you and inspire you to tackle the unknown. Such a friend will prove professionally invaluable.

Learn from your actions. Harvard Business School's John Kotter suggests, "You grab a challenge, act on it, then honestly reflect on why your actions worked or didn't. You learn from it and then move on. That continuous process of lifelong learning helps enormously in a rapidly changing economic environment."

I read about two guys who should have heeded the advice to learn from their actions. Jake and Joe were avid hunters. A week of hunting in the backwoods of Canada netted them each a large moose. When their pilot returned to retrieve them from the wilderness, he had an immediate concern. "I can't fly you out of here with all the gear and those two moose."

"Why not?" asked a surprised Joe.

"Because my plane doesn't have enough horsepower to carry such a load."

"But the plane that flew us out of here last year was exactly like this one," Jake protested.

"Really?" the pilot responded. "Well, I guess if you did it last year, I can do it, too."

They loaded the plane and began their takeoff. The plane crept across the water but struggled to climb out of the forest with all the weight and crashed into the mountain side.

Shaken but uninjured, the men crawled from the wreckage and Joe asked, "Where are we?"

Jake surveyed the surroundings and replied, "I'm not sure, but I guess we are about a mile farther than last year."

Learn from your experiences. If things don't work, don't keep doing them the same way, and expect positive results.

Today's organization has no pity on the person who is lackadaisical about learning. People are expected to take responsibility for updating their skills or be left in the dust. Becoming obsolete happens quickly without constant retooling. Your supervisor may be a great advocate for personal growth, but you will ultimately need to jump-start the internal drive to stay abreast of what's needed for you to acquire the necessary specialized knowledge. The more you know, the more valuable you become.

Eric Hofer believed, "In time of drastic change, it is the learners who inherit the future. The learned usually find themselves equipped to live in a world that no longer exists." Prepare now to be ready for your inheritance . . . the future.

GROW BEYOND WHERE
YOU ARE

Only those who
constantly
retool
themselves
stand a chance
of staying
employed in the
years ahead.
TOM PETERS

❊

pdate your résumé. List all of your skills, talents, and unique abilities. Include both your personal and professional qualities. Don't break your arm patting yourself on the back, but do take time to review the achievements you've experienced.

Now, based on what you've written, ask yourself the following question: What have I done in the past 30 days to increase my competence in these areas and expand my capabilities?

The fulfilled professional and the one considered the most valuable by employers is an ever-growing, always expanding individual. Think beyond the basics you have mastered to new opportunities and challenges. Instead of locking your radar into a comfort zone, pursue the unknown. Gain insight into areas others have overlooked. Become inquisitive by exploring options for innovative changes and improvements.

Resting on past achievements is no longer acceptable and far from guaranteeing a promising career. Constant upgrading of skills is required to face the changing nature of the world around us. Job security isn't earned by showing up. We need to reformat our thinking around the value we offer to the organization. Feeling entitled to climbing another rung on the ladder, salary increases, or even maintaining our present positions is a defeating trap.

Become an expert at what you do. Constant retooling—perpetual learning—professional renewal—These are the tools of a marketable and competent professional. A relentless drive to effect work habits, improve your credentials, delve deeper into your interests, and maintain a thirst for never finishing your education.

My daughter is a dancer. I marvel at the effort it takes for her to achieve new levels of dance precision. Practice involves stretching muscles, coordinating graceful steps and distinct arm movements, pushing her limits, and all the while producing a smile that camouflages her discomfort.

The year-end dance recital creates excitement and anticipation for the performers to display the fruits of their efforts. Grueling hours of instruction and learning culminate into a parent-pleasing production. But none of this is possible without incremental, consistent growth.

Your recital is a daily performance that requires you to dream, dare, stretch, and risk outside the ordinary habitual ambitions. Don't let the past or present competencies evolve into future inadequacies. Work through the discomfort that often accompanies stretching. Remind yourself daily that the more you challenge yourself to expand beyond the customary comfort box, the easier your task will be when called upon to perform a crowd-pleasing production.

A friend asked Henry Wadsworth Longfellow the secret of his continued interest in life. Pointing to a nearby apple tree, he responded, "The purpose of that apple tree is to grow a little new wood each year. That is what I plan to do." I can handle professional growth when understood from Longfellow's perspective. Growing a little new wood each year protects us from stagnation and might even prompt us to grow a whole new branch.

Excelling requires us to move beyond past limitations and the present *status quo*. Reinvest your energies in the undiscovered, uncharted, unusual way of doing things.

Abandon the familiar ruts and overcome your addiction to ineffective ways of doing things. Create a new performance paradigm that yields a shift in the way you've always approached your job.

The more you know, the more you know how to do, the better you do it, the more valuable you become, and the more career satisfaction you'll attain.

As long as you're green, you're growing; as soon as you're ripe, you start to rot.

RAY KROC

PREPARE FOR
THE FUTURE

*The pace of
events is
moving so fast
that unless we
can find some
way to keep
our sights on
tomorrow, we
cannot expect
to be in touch
with today.*

DEAN RUSK

❋

The story is told of a man who realized he was slowly losing his memory. He sought the counsel of a doctor and, after a careful examination, the doctor said that an operation on his brain might reverse his condition and restore his memory. "However," the doctor said, "you must understand how delicate this surgery is. If one nerve is severed, total blindness could result."

A deafening silence filled the room.

"What would you rather have," asked the surgeon, attempting to break the uncomfortable silence, "your sight or your memory?"

The man pondered his choices for a few moments and then replied, "My sight, because I would rather see where I am going than remember where I have been."

This same mindset is endorsed by the person who understands how fast life is moving and, in order to survive and thrive, must move beyond the past. You can't forget your past but neither do you have to live in it. Jack Hayford, pastor of Church of the Way in Van Nuys, California commented, "The past is a dead issue, and we can't gain any momentum moving toward tomorrow if we are dragging the past behind us." As important as your past is, it is not so important as the way you see and prepare for the future. Therefore, our efforts should be directed toward refining our vision, not saving our memory.

Here are helpful hints for building your future:

Know what you stand for. I've encountered a lot of people in recent years who are troubled about tomorrow. People worry about what's coming next. What will they have to face? How can they measure up to increasing demands? How can they keep their lives on track?

Carrying around such heavy concerns can become a real burden. One anecdote for these anxieties is to know exactly for what you stand. What values and principles guide your life? Where are you willing to be flexible? In what areas is there no room for negotiation? Be clear about the boundaries that will provide a clear path for you to live your life.

Double-check your perspective. Where there is no hope in the future, we remain obsessed with the past. Where there is faith in the future, there is power to live today.

Fear is certainly a normal emotion when we look ahead. That's one reason why a lot of people keep living in the past. What's there to fear, I've already endured it all. There are a lot of uncontrollable variables when you begin anticipating tomorrow. But it is tomorrow where we will spend the rest of our lives and it is unhealthy and unnecessary to let fear remain in control.

There is a definite fascination with pointing out the inevitable downside of the future. I never cease to be amazed at the number of people who can catastrophize the smallest bad news into this generation's major depression. Dr. Norman Cousins advised, "One of the most important things in life is the need *not* to accept downside predictions from experts. It's true in interpersonal relationships just as it is true in business. No one knows enough to make a pronouncement of doom."

It's antiproductive to complain about possible future events. Substantial energy is lost resisting, being angry, or avoiding a future that challenges present assumptions and expectations. Maintain the faith, see the bigger picture, and invest your energies to seize potential opportunities.

Be flexible. Somebody once said, "Blessed are the flexible, for they shall not be bent out of shape." Here's a bit of advice that should go without saying, but it bears repeating: Be prepared that not everything in life will go according to your plan.

Considerable disappointment could be averted if people would look for new approaches when things don't go their way. Rather than bemoaning the unfairness of life, invest your energy in finding and seizing previously nonexistent, priceless opportunities. By catching on to this principle, you'll be better able to remain caught up with the pace of change.

Allow the virtues of hard work and positive anticipation to create a renewed sense of hope for future success.

Focus on a vision for the future. Fasten your seat belt. This step is going to take a fast track to some serious thought control and adjustment. Instead of worrying about or bemoaning all that could happen, get busy creating a vision of the future you want.

Peter Block, writing in *The Empowered Manager,* reminds us that, "We claim ownership over our lives when we identify the future that we want for ourselves and our unit. Our deepest commitment is to choose to live, to choose the destiny that has been handed to us, and to choose to pursue that destiny. These choices are expressed at work when we create a vision for our unit and decide to pursue that vision at all costs."

You will be far happier if you put the future to work for you rather than allowing the future to work you. Make next week, next year, and the coming decade your ally by determining what you want and setting your sights on achieving it. Keep the vision continually in front of you, review it frequently in your imagination, and determine specific actions that will move you closer each day.

In an essay entitled "Good Guys Finish First (Sometimes)," Andrew Bagnato told the following story:

Following a rags-to-riches season that led them to the Rose Bowl—their first in decades—Northwestern University's Wildcats met with coach Gary Barnett for the opening of spring training.

As players found their seats, Barnett announced that he was going to hand out the awards that many Wildcats had earned in 1995. Some players exchanged glances. Barnett does not normally dwell on the past. But as the coach continued to call players forward and handed them placards proclaiming their achievements, they were cheered on by their teammates.

One of the other coaches gave Barnett a placard representing his 17 national coach-of-the-year awards. Then, as the applause subsided, Barnett walked to a trash can marked "1995." He took an admiring glance at his placard, then dumped it in the can.

In the silence that followed, one by one, the team's stars dumped their placards on top of Barnett's. Barnett had shouted a message without uttering a word: "What you did in 1995 was terrific, lads. But look at the calendar: It's 1996."

André Gide suggested, "One doesn't discover new lands without consenting to lose sight of the shore for a very long time." Put the shore of yesterday behind you and begin stretching for a new horizon.

Today is the first day of the rest of your life. So, it's no use fussing about the past because you can't do anything about it. But you have today, and today is when everything that's going to happen from now on begins.

HARVEY FIRESTONE, JR.

SETTLE FOR NOTHING LESS THAN WOW!

Do what you do so well that those who see you do what you do are going to come back to see you do it again and tell others that they should see what you do.

WALT DISNEY

❈

To achieve a level of "Wow" performance requires you to be more than average. You must go beyond what anyone would expect. Henry Ward Beecher believed that to achieve success, "Hold yourself responsible for a higher standard than anybody else expects of you."

"No one ever attains very eminent success by simply doing what is required of him," added Charles Kendall Adams. "It is the amount and excellence of what is over and above the required that determines greatness." Let me illustrate.

As a young father, Walt Disney would accompany his daughters on afternoon getaways to a local amusement park. While sitting on a dirty park bench, indulging in stale popcorn, rubbery hot dogs, and watered-down drinks, he dreamed of creating the ideal amusement park. He dreamed of a place where families around the world would be attracted to visit. From Mainstreet USA, to Pirates of the Caribbean, Disney thought through every intricate detail.

Quality food, cleanliness, attractive and inviting rides, and a variety of wholesome entertainment would be fun for everyone. This would be a family adventure second to none.

It took Walt 15 years to make his dream a reality. Even those closest to Disney found it hard to relate to his expansive vision. His own brother, Roy, thought the entire concept was a screwball idea. Walt encountered numerous obstacles and problems. It would have been easy to settle for something less than the ideal. But by the time Disneyland opened in 1955, the real thing was just as impressive as he had pictured it.

Thirty thousand people visited Disneyland on opening day. By the end of seven weeks, one million people had enjoyed Disney's creation. Today millions of people each year experience the fulfillment of Disney's own admonition: "Do what you do so well that those who see you do what you do are going to come back to see you do it again and tell others that they should see what you do."

Disney knew that if he didn't create a "Wow" experience, people would forget Disneyland existed and it would soon be considered just another run-of-the-mill amusement park. To avoid such a demise, the brass on

Disneyland's carousel is polished daily, the park benches always appear new due to frequent applications of paint, and the shooting gallery targets get a paint touch-up every night. The cleaning crew is extensively trained before assuming their incredible challenge and even the car parking crew is thoroughly instructed on Disney's commitment to courtesy.

No doubt about it, Walt Disney raised the bar on amusement park expectations. He began with a lofty vision of what could be, and persevered in selling that vision and the tangible result. Disney paid very close attention to details and challenged developers to continually find ways to improve on the design. His own personal high standards and self-discipline made it possible for those carrying on after him to create a "Wow" experience.

Willa A. Foster once said, "Quality is never an accident; it is always the result of high intention, sincere effort, intelligent direction, and skillful execution; it represents the wise choice of many alternatives." Simply stated: You will only be as good as the choices you make. Talent, circumstances, luck, heredity, environment, and personality are immaterial. What matters is how good you plan to be using what you have.

Personal and professional excellence requires 100 percent all the time. A passionate commitment 89, 93, or even 98 percent of the time reduces the "Wow" factor to acceptable or mediocre. Adequacy is an unstimulating goal to attain. If you want others to notice your efforts, make plans to do it better than you or they ever thought possible.

"No matter what you do, do it to your utmost," advised Russell H. Conwell. "I always attribute my success . . . to always requiring myself to do my level best, if only in driving a tack in straight." Enough said.

Successful people never settle for mediocrity or not using their abilities to the fullest. Zig Ziglar said, "Success is the maximum utilization of the ability that you have." Legendary basketball coach John Wooden concurs. "Success," he said, "comes from knowing that you did your best to become the best that you are capable of becoming." In that pursuit, it is impossible to be satisfied with anything less than excellence.

Since the day our children were old enough to understand, we instituted a cardinal rule in our home. It wasn't always a popular rule because it held the children accountable for their actions. The rule? Approach every ball game, school

My philosophy is that not only are you responsible for your life, but doing the best at this moment puts you in the best place for the next moment.

OPRAH WINFREY

challenge, dance competition, musical performance, or any other day-to-day life experience with a sincere commitment to give your best. My wife and I never required our children to be the best, the smartest, or the fastest. However, they would tell you there was an inexcusable expectation that they would give, perform, and be the best they could be.

Remember Nadia Comaneci? She was the first gymnast ever to earn a perfect score in Olympic competition. I remember watching that flawless performance during the 1976 Olympics in Montreal. It was impossible not to get excited about her performance and the gold medal.

In a later interview, Comaneci explained the expectations she set for herself and how she was able to maintain such a high standard of performance: "I always underestimated what I did by saying, 'I can do better.' To be an Olympic champion you have to be a little abnormal and work harder than everyone else. Being normal is not great because you will have a boring life. I live by a code I created: Don't pray for an easy life. Pray to be a strong person."

Successful people go beyond what others consider acceptable. They do more than others expect, set standards that stretch them beyond their last performance, pay attention to the smallest details, and are willing to go the extra mile that pushes them outside the box of mediocrity. Being your best never happens by accident. You have to make it happen and that begins with an attitude that accepts personal responsibility for the methods and results you experience.

Sometimes I worry about being a success in a mediocre world.

LILY TOMLIN

BECOME THE "OWN" IN OWNERSHIP

*The secret to success on the job is to work
as though you were working for yourself.
Your company provides you with the work area,
equipment and other benefits, but basically you
know what has to get done
and the best way to do it, so it's up to
you to run your own show.*

LAIR RIBEIRO

Success Is No Accident

ACT LIKE
AN OWNER

Calculate the hours you spend at work, and you'll quickly realize your job represents a major part of your life. It requires a huge investment, so working for just a paycheck and a few benefits will provide only temporary work enjoyment. In fact, one of the worst mistakes you can make is to think you are working for someone else.

Andy Grove, Intel Corporation's CEO, gave a group of graduates from the University of California at Berkeley some sound advice. He said, "Accept that no matter where you go to work, you are not an employee—you are a business with one employee, you. Nobody owes you a career. You own it, as a sole proprietor. You must compete with millions of individuals every day of your career. You must enhance your value every day, hone your competitive advantage, learn, adapt, move jobs and industries—retrench so you can advance, learn new skills. So you do not become one of those

Always accept yourself as self-employed and look upon every single thing you accomplish or don't accomplish as your own responsibility.
BRIAN TRACY

statistics in 2015. And remember: This process starts on Monday."

Here's how you can activate an ownership lifestyle. Assume the presidency of your own personal corporation. Accept responsibility for the results you generate and continually seek resolutions to performance problems and productivity barriers. A natural outcome will be that your performance advances to the next level. You are ultimately accountable for the quality of your work and the fulfillment you experience. Challenge yourself to do whatever it takes to be successful and take responsibility for failures. No matter who signs your paycheck, in the final analysis, you work for yourself.

Invest yourself passionately in what you do. There is no room in today's marketplace for people who punch in, half-heartedly go through eight hours of repetitive motions, and punch out. Take charge of your morale. Don't depend on the organization or someone else to pump you up. No one possesses the power to keep you inspired. Fill your own energy tank. Immersed in what you do as an owner, you create a unique capacity to enjoy the adventure of work for extended periods of time.

Never confuse longevity with contribution. Tenure is important if you continue to add value to your department and/or the organization. I feel sorry for people who live under the mistaken assumption that longevity qualifies them for security, additional salary, or added privileges. It just doesn't work that way. Organizations simply don't take the personal interest in people's careers like they did in the past. Most of us are primarily on our own.

Loyalty to your company is valuable but you don't get extra credit for "putting in your time." Look outside your job description to find ways to contribute more to the organization than you cost. Do more than you are asked. Stay later than is expected of you. Search for ways to increase your worth to the organization far beyond what you are being paid. Make it evident that you would be missed if you weren't there. If you can't identify specific things you have done to profit your company in this way, get your résumé updated.

Think in terms of partnership. J.C. Penney once declared, "I will have no man work for me who has not the capacity to become a partner." Inspire other people to make things happen. Look for ways to cultivate cooperative relationships. Assume more personal responsibility for the success of the entire organization. Create a vision of what your department could become. How can you personally cut costs, improve productivity, eliminate waste, serve the customer better, and improve the emotional well-being of the company?

Embrace the demands of change. Organizations need high-performance people. It is virtually impossible to stay on the cutting-edge of your profession without continual, and, oftentimes, rapid growth. Become a master at what you do and then do whatever it takes to stay abreast of what is happening in your field. The choice is to either be a perpetual student who continually acquires new skills or become outdated and obsolete.

Learn to deal with ambiguity and uncertainty. Pro-actively endorse shifting and expanding responsibilities. Remain fluid and flexible. Improvise as necessary and accept the fact that times are changing and things are not returning to "normal." Feel your way down the path to the future and remain answerable for your actions. Become self-empowered. Discover your untapped potential.

Behaving like you're in business for yourself frees you to capitalize on possibilities and be accountable for outcomes. This is a marvelous opportunity to shine in your position, develop an entrepreneurial reputation, and make a significant difference for those who pay for your work.

TAKE THE TIME TO
FIX YOUR LEAKY BOAT

The rule of accuracy: When working toward the solution of a problem it always helps if you know the answer.

JOHN PEER

❀

Here's some news you'll love to hear: Problems are a part of every job. Of course, that's nothing new to you. What's important is whether you decide to do something about your problems or just be satisfied to complain about them. It's easy to get so caught up in your trials and tribulations that you fail to get beyond them.

I love the story of a man in a rowboat about 25 yards offshore. He's rowing like crazy but getting nowhere. A woman standing on the nearby shore sees the man is in trouble and notices the rowboat has a bad leak and is slowly sinking. She shouts to the man, but he's too busy bailing water to answer her. She shouts louder; he continues to row and bail. Finally she yells at the top of her lungs, "Hey, if you don't get the boat ashore and fix the leak, you're going to drown!"

"Thanks, lady," the man replies, "but I don't have time to fix the leak."

We all encounter situations when it takes every ounce of energy we have just to stay afloat. Bailing and rowing become the dominant activities. If we would only take the time to fix the source of our problem, rather than just desperately attack the symptoms, we might not be so worn out at the end of the day. Every job requires us to go ashore periodically to fix our leaky boats.

Problems are as natural as the sun coming up in the morning and going down at night. You'll see plenty of them in your career. Build a reputation as a problem-solver, and you'll be considered a valuable person on the team. Here are a few strategies to consider as you become a leak fixer.

Admit there is a leak. "Stubbornness in refusing to recognize a problem has destroyed a lot of bottom lines," observed Harvey Mackay. "You can't solve a problem unless you first admit you have one."

In his book *Identity: Youth and Crisis,* Erik Erikson tells a story he got from a physician about a man with a peculiar situation. The old man vomited every morning but had never felt any inclination to consult a doctor. Finally, the man's family convinced him to get checked out.

The doctor asked, "How are you?"

"I'm fine," the man responded. "Couldn't be better."

The doctor examined him and found he was in good shape for his age. Finally, the physician grew impatient and asked, "I hear that you vomit every morning."

The old man looked surprised and said, "Sure. Doesn't everybody?"

Some people don't realize the problems they live with are abnormal. They have been dealing with them for so long, they've convinced themselves that everyone has a leaky boat.

"Recognizing a problem doesn't always bring a solution," James Baldwin reminds us, "but until we recognize that problem, there can be no solution."

Be realistic about the size of the hole. Many times people look at a problem telescopically so the leak looks bigger than it actually is. As E.W. Howe wrote in *Success Is Easier Than Failure,* "Some people storm imaginary Alps all their lives, and die in the foothills cursing difficulties that do not exist." Out of such instances arose the popular "don't make a mountain out of a molehill" advice. American publisher Al Neuharth said, "The difference between a mountain and a molehill is your perspective."

A businessperson experienced a drastic downturn in sales, and the possibility of shutting down was a real threat. When a friend asked how he was doing, the man replied, "Times are so tough I'm getting several calls a day from national leaders."

The friend was taken back a bit and asked, "Why are they calling you?"

The down-in-the-mouth executive replied, "They enjoy talking with someone who has bigger problems than they do."

John Maxwell believes, "People need to change their perspectives, not their problems." Don't exaggerate the enormity of your problems. Overreacting or "catastrophizing" puts the power in the problem rather than your ability to solve it. Be suspicious of the power and control you've given any challenge.

Don't wait for a lifeguard. Accept responsibility for the problems you are experiencing and you can begin to rise above the crisis. Wait for a lifeguard to rescue you, and you may drown before help arrives.

A critical mistake many people make is assigning fault for a problem and then removing themselves from any responsibility for resolving it. If you're in the boat and the boat springs a leak, whose problem is it? Even though the leak might have been created by someone else, it would be wise for you to make some adjustments or be willing to accept the annoyances, conflict, or drowning the leak will cause.

A problem is something you can do something about. If you fail to do something about it, it will become a fact of life and then you will need to learn to live with it. Because we've gotten so good at the blame game and avoiding personal responsibility, we've become victims by our own choices.

Comedian and actor W.C. Fields once said, "Remember, a dead fish can float downstream, but it takes a live one to swim upstream." It takes minimal effort or skill to point an accusing finger at other people. What difference does it make now to blame others? The problem is yours and is in need of corrective action.

The truly effective person is the one who can navigate upstream, against the flow of irresponsibility and finger-pointing, toward workable solutions. It's your boat you're sitting in. Take ownership for its condition. Don't focus on the leak. That only produces fear, anger, desperation, or paralysis. Trapped in those emotional reactions, the clarity of the ideal solution is blurred. Tap into your experience and insight to discover how best to solve the leak.

Find a plug that fills the hole. I love the story of the old country doctor who was giving a patient an examination. At the conclusion, he scratched his head and asked in bewilderment, "Have you had this before?"

"Yes, I have," the patient replied.

The doctor looked his patient in the eye and said, "Well, you've got it again."

The epitome of frustration comes from the continual analysis of a problem without a proper diagnosis and plan of action. You can stare at a hole in the boat and repeat to yourself over and over, "Yep, there's a hole in the boat," but until a course of correction is set, this risk of sinking remains.

John Foster Dulles, Secretary of State during the Eisenhower administration, suggested that, "The measure of success is not whether you have a tough problem to deal with, but whether it's the same problem you had last year." Thomas J. Watson, Jr., former head of IBM, said, "I never varied from the managerial rule that the worst possible thing we could do would be to lie dead in the water with any problem. Solve it, solve it quickly, solve it right or wrong. If you solved it wrong, it would come back and slap you in the face and then you could solve it right. Doing nothing is a comfortable alternative because it is without immediate risk, but it is an absolutely fatal way to manage a business."

Pastor and author A.B. Simpson told the story of a farmer who plowed around a large rock in his field year after year. He had broken several pieces of equipment by running into it. Each time he saw that rock sprawled out in his field, he grumbled about how much trouble it had caused.

One day the farmer decided to dig up the rock and do away with it for good. Putting a large crowbar under one side, he began prying and soon discovered, much to his surprise, that the rock was less than a foot thick. Within a short period of time, he had removed the rock from the field and hauled it away in his wagon. He smiled to think how that "monstrous" rock had caused him so much frustration.

Quit plowing around your problems. They will still be there tomorrow. We don't need the same old problems reoccurring day after day after day. New challenges are continually coming your way and the cumulative affect of new and old problems can be overwhelming. Sigmund Freud stated, "A man with a toothache cannot be in love." Why? Because he spends all his time thinking about the toothache.

Dispose of the old hassles. Work through them. Search for alternative approaches. Make some decisions. Find solutions. Take care of them so you can move on to new opportunities.

Understand the value of leaks. Problems are a natural, inevitable condition for growth. All growth produces problems but not all problems produce growth. The difference is your understanding of that truth. Lloyd Ogilvie, writing in his book *If God Cares, Why Do I Still Have Problems,* suggests, "The greatest problem we all share, to a greater or lesser degree, is a profound misunderstanding of the positive purpose of problems. Until we grapple with this gigantic problem, we will be helpless victims of our problems all through our life."

Problems are a source of instruction, insight, and opportunity. When we learn to look at them correctly, the challenge of meeting those problems head on keeps us alive, vibrant, and on our toes. Problems stimulate the development of our mind and talents while stretching us to new levels of thinking and performance. Reacting foolishly, resenting problems, or avoiding them will keep you from experiencing the benefits they can bring.

The best way to eat the elephant standing in your path is to cut it up into little pieces.

AFRICAN
PROVERB

❀

In *The Road Less Traveled,* best-selling author Scott Peck offers this valuable perspective on problems: "It is in this whole process of meeting and solving problems that life has meaning. Problems are the cutting edge that distinguishes between success and failure. Problems call forth our courage and our wisdom; indeed they create our courage and our wisdom. It is only because of problems that we grow mentally and spiritually. It is through the pain of confronting and resolving problems that we learn. As Benjamin Franklin said, 'Those things that hurt, instruct.'"

Look with an open mind for the value in each challenge you encounter. Every miracle in the Bible began with a problem. So, when you find yourself surrounded by water in your leaking boat, implement the suggestions you've just read and keep in mind that you are a candidate for a miracle.

DON'T HOLD
BACK

I realize that no matter what anyone says, some people will always embrace Mark Twain's attitude when he said, "I do not like work even when someone else does it." However, I'm also convinced that most of us are interested in erasing any possibility for a vague and undefined work life. The simple fact is, we want more than a paycheck.

I predict there are very few people in the world who get up in the morning, shower, dress, have a little breakfast, and announce, "I can't wait to do a really *bad* job today."

Yet, surveys indicate nearly 85 percent of the workers in the United States say they could work harder on the job, and nearly half claim they could double their effectiveness.

Too many people are not emotionally committed to the importance of what they do. The job is often blamed but that is absurd. For every person complaining about his or her job, there are several others investing themselves in those perceived mundane experiences.

> *There's a difference between interest and commitment. When you're interested in doing something, you do it only when it is convenient. When you are committed to something, you accept no excuses, only results.*
>
> KEN BLANCHARD
>

Every organization has people who always do less than they are told; still others who will do what they are told, but no more; and some who will do things without being told. What organizations need more of is the minority group who actually inspire others to do things. These are people who constantly renew their own commitment to being their best.

The world has little room for people who put in their time, go through the motions with a half-hearted effort, and are careless, sloppy, or even indifferent. A grand prize for showing up and going through the motions is not in the cards. The uncommitted are left in the dust.

In today's world, people who eliminate excuses, pro-actively work from the heart, invest themselves passionately in what they do, and apply their skills and talents to the fullest are maximizing their professional potential.

President Eisenhower, while addressing the National Press Club, opened his remarks by apologizing that he was not a great orator. He likened his situation to a boyhood experience on a Kansas farm.

Eisenhower recalled, "An old farmer had a cow that we wanted to buy. We went over to visit him and asked about the cow's pedigree. The old farmer didn't know what pedigree meant, so we asked him about the cow's butterfat production. He told us that he hadn't any idea. Finally, we asked him if he knew how many pounds of milk the cow produced each year. The farmer shook his head and said, 'I don't know. But she's an honest old cow and she'll give you all the milk she has!'"

Eisenhower then concluded his opening remarks, "Well, I'm like the cow: I'll give you everything I have."

That is a pure and simple commitment. When the urge to slough off arises or you're on the verge of giving less than your best, consider Eisenhower's pledge. Giving everything you have makes work far more satisfying. It's a great anecdote for boredom as well as stress and is ultimately a gift you give to yourself.

Commitment unlocks the doors of imagination, allows vision and gives us the 'right stuff' to turn our dreams into reality.

JAMES WOMACK

GIVE YOUR BEST
TO WHAT
MATTERS MOST

*Time only runs in one direction and seems
to do so in an orderly fashion.*

PATRICIA CORNWELL

TAKE A FEW MINUTES
TO THINK ABOUT TIME

Bernard Benson once commented, "I wish I could stand on a busy corner, hat in hand, and beg people to throw me all their wasted hours." There's a good chance he'd become a wealthy man given the opportunity to fulfill his wish. I doubt there is anything people waste more of than time.

Time-management expert Michael Fortino launched an in-depth study called the Fortino Efficiency Index. Fortino discovered that during the course of a lifetime, the average American spends . . .

- One year looking for misplaced objects
- Eight months opening junk mail
- Two years trying to return phone calls of people who never seem to be in
- Five years standing in line (at the bank, movie theater, etc.)

Additional research by Tor Dahl, chairperson of the World Confederation of Productivity Science, indicates that the average American business wastes or misdirects work time as follows:

- 23 percent waiting for approvals, materials, or support
- 20 percent doing things that shouldn't even be done
- 15 percent doing things that should be handled by someone else
- 18 percent doing things wrong
- 16 percent for failing to do the right things

Do any of those sound familiar? You can probably list additional daily activities that rob you of valuable time. Just being aware of and sensitive to avoiding wasted minutes and hours can provide a fresh perspective of time.

My intent is not to offer a cure-all for the epidemic of lost time. I am interested in offering you an assorted selection of antibiotics you can draw on to treat this infection. Although our lack of effectiveness and efficiency can be hindered by a number of external infecting agents, we are ultimately responsible for dealing with the causes and symptoms. Time is your personal possession. Nobody can manage it or fix it for you. You are in control. You can do something. Your life is yours and you can choose to live it with greater control and healthy time usage.

You might be plagued with a lack of self discipline, indecisiveness, or even personal disorganization. Maybe the cause of time slipping by is daydreaming, poor delegation skills, an inability to say no, or a lack of priorities. Whatever the case, here is a plethora of ideas for you to consider. Give immediate attention to those that cause an "Aha" reaction.

1. Ask the right question. First and foremost, when involved in any activity that hints of wasted time, ask yourself, "Is this the best way for me to be spending my time right now?" Then, act accordingly.

2. Schedule work according to your peak productivity time. Designate those hours you are most productive to doing things that give the highest return and produce the greatest value. The German poet Goethe put it this way: "The key to life is concentration and elimination."

3. Determine your priorities. You can't do everything. Overambitious to-do lists can be unrealistic and antiproductive. Make choices. Sort out your "have-to's" from your "choose-to's." You'll be amazed how many times you choose to do rather than have to do. Direct your energies toward activities that are the most important to you.

Robert Eliot suggested, "It's important to run not on the fast track, but on your track. Pretend you only have six months to live, and make three lists: the things you *have* to do, *want* to do, and neither have to do nor want to do. Then, for the rest of your life, forget everything on the third list."

4. Be result oriented rather than activity oriented. Activity does not equal accomplishment. "No other principle of effectiveness is violated as constantly today as the basic principle of concentration," said Peter Drucker. "Our motto seems to be, 'let's do a little bit of everything.'" Measure your effectiveness by what you achieve, not by how busy you are.

5. Get organized. According to Albert R. Karr, writing in the *Wall Street Journal,* "Executives waste nearly six weeks a year looking for misplaced items, according to a poll of 200 large-company executives for Accountemps, a temporary help firm." Have a place for everything, and have everything in its place.

6. Get up earlier. By rising 30 minutes earlier each day, you add 3-½ hours of productivity to your week. Multiply that by 52 weeks and you'll have an additional 180 hours to accomplish your priorities. I've used these extra hours to write books, design seminars, and get energized spiritually by reading inspirational material or spending time in prayer.

7. Learn to say no. Busy people must simply learn to refuse some demands made on their time. It's natural not to want to disappoint people. Sometimes we're unrealistic about our limits. It's easy to let our ego get in the way of saying no; the need to be needed is a powerful decision influence. You'll never feel in control if you're biting off more than you can chew.

8. Work on your attitude. Your attitude about how busy you are, the amount of time you have, or the demands on your life can sabotage any effort to make the most of the time you have. Be flexible. Not everything will go as expected. Seek new opportunities when your game plan runs into road blocks.

9. Quit daydreaming. Turn mind wandering into action.

10. Do things right the first time. If you don't have time to do it right, when will you have time to do it over?

11. Plan ahead. For instance, lay your clothes out for the next day before you go to bed at night, purchase holiday or birthday presents in advance, and keep tabs on special days and events 30 days in advance.

12. Place deadlines on yourself. Don't allow minor or major projects to drag on indefinitely. Challenge yourself with deadlines, and beat them.

13. Prepare for unexpected down time. Spare minutes created by waiting in airports, restaurants, traffic, etc., can be the perfect time to indulge in small projects.

14. Manage meetings. Use a specific time like 9:13 or 1:32 to start your meetings and set a predetermined time for adjournment. Stay on task.

15. Don't put off until the day after tomorrow what you can do today. Procrastination is an ugly, frustrating habit. Do it today.

The philosopher and poet Goethe said, "We have time enough if we will but use it aright." Time is a precious commodity. It is available to all of us in equal parts to use as we choose. Time is like a talent—you can't produce more of it but you can make the most of what you have. To get the most out of each day, learn to savor each moment and make the most of every hour. Now would be a good time to take a minute to evaluate how you spend your hours.

Don't put off for tomorrow what you can do today, because if you enjoy it today, you can do it again tomorrow.

JAMES A. MICHENER

LEARN TO SCHEDULE
YOUR PRIORITIES

The reason most major goals are not achieved is that we spend our time doing second things first.

ROBERT MCKAIN

Notice the title doesn't read "prioritize your schedule." Instead, decide what you want to spend your time doing. What are the most important elements of your life and work? Establish your priorities and then stick to them. Schedule them into your routine.

Unless you live congruently with your priorities, you will never feel in balance. You'll always have that nagging feeling that you're in a rat race you can't win. Awareness of and commitment to our priorities increases performance and productivity. With increasing forces pulling us in every direction, this principle is more important than ever.

Allow sufficient time and energy to enjoy the experiences, people, and activities you value most. This is the simplest yet most profound foundation for a successful life. All other goals and strategies for attaining them will fall into place when you live by the values you profess.

Don't be tempted or driven by distractions. Jumping from one thing to the next is the result of an undisciplined commitment to priorities. You don't have the emotional resources or physical energy to sufficiently support every worthy ideal vying for your attention.

Each day we are given the gift of 24 hours—1,440 minutes—86,400 seconds. Only one person can decide how this gift will be used. However we decide to invest our time communicates to others the values we espouse. You may argue that is not true of you. I would challenge you to consider this question: "Am I satisfied with the amount and quality of time I am giving to the important priorities in my life?" Don't immediately answer that, but ponder it for a few days.

Whenever we decide to do one thing, we have made a decision not to give our attention to something else. Time management, or life management for that matter, is a series of choices.

My fascination with the circus led me to discover the secret of the lion tamer's success. I found that, along with the whip and pistol strapped to his belt, the lion tamer's key tool is a four-legged stool. The stool is held by the back and the legs are thrust toward the face of the lion. Apparently the wild animal attempts to focus on all four legs at once, thereby overwhelming its senses. The lion is left paralyzed, tamed, and unable to aggressively respond. Sound familiar? Focus. Focus. Focus.

What are the top five personal priorities in your life? What are your five most important professional responsibilities? Now evaluate how much time you have given to each in the past six months. Are the hours and days adding up to the quality of life you desire?

If sufficient time and energy have been allocated for these priorities, you probably sense a degree of balance. Life feels in sync. If, on the other hand, these priorities are pushed on the back burner, I would wager there is a feeling of incompleteness and dissatisfaction.

Please note the wording of this strategy. I'm not suggesting a prioritizing of all daily responsibilities, activities, and events. Rather, based on your purpose, determine your top personal and professional priorities. Now schedule them into your weekly calendar. Religiously make sure these priorities are given top billing.

Most people don't have trouble listing their priorities. Few people seem to be able to give sufficient time to them.

We have good intentions. We make a gallant effort for a few weeks, but then tend to fall back into the habit of allowing our calendars to dictate our priorities, and soon life is out of sync.

I was involved in a greenhouse operation that raised 2,800 tomato plants. For us to raise the highest quality tomatoes took considerable maintenance. Little shoots at the bottom of the plant had to be trimmed or they would drain nutrients from the main stem. By trimming the "suckers," the remainder of the plant receives proper nourishment, thereby producing luscious fruit.

Our automatic watering system insured each plant received sufficient moisture to keep it healthy. Without the water, the plants would shrivel up and die. We had the labor and nutritional resources to support each plant.

Snip off your time suckers. Let them go. Nourish the fruit-producing priorities. Give them your energetic attention and celebrate the results.

Donald Rumsfeld suggested: "Control your own time. Don't let it be done for you. If you are working on the in-box that is fed you, you are probably working on the priority of others." Put into action today a plan that will allow you to choose how the precious gift of time will be spent.

Things that matter most must never be at the mercy of things that matter least.

JOHANN WOLFGANG VON GOETHE

I KNOW YOU'RE BUSY,
BUT WHAT ARE YOU GETTING DONE?

Do not tell me how hard you work. Tell me how much you get done.

JAMES J. LING

Our high school Spanish Club sold candy to raise money for a trip to Mexico. The sponsoring teacher reminded each student how important it was to contact as many people as possible about buying the candy. "We've got ten days to make this fund-raiser successful," the teacher instructed. "I want to know at the end of those ten days how many contacts you made. Good luck."

As the students brought in their orders, one girl was bragging about her success. "I called on 74 houses door to door in one night. I started right after school and didn't even stop for supper. I would have been able to do more but a couple of people stopped me and wanted to buy."

In our fast-paced world it is easy to get caught up in a fury of activity. Observe people around you. Some are rushing here and there, attending one meeting after another, attempting to concentrate on several activities or projects at one time, writing reports, talking on the phone, eating on the run, and accomplishing very little.

The world doesn't care, whether you like it or not, how busy you are. The world doesn't reward you for how smart you are, your good intentions, or the dreams you hope to pursue.

What's important are results, what you have actually done. Far too often, we pat ourselves on the back for running in place even though the finish line is as far away at the end of the day as when we started the day. People who get things done will reap more than a self-appreciating pat on the back.

Making the transformation from being one who dilly-dallies throughout the day to one who makes a contribution involves an evaluation of current activity. Henry Ford said, "The number of needless tasks that are performed daily by thousands of people is amazing." He had a list of them, including:

- They make too many phone calls.

- They visit too often and stay too long on each visit.

- They write letters that are three times as long as necessary.

- They work on little things, neglect big ones.
- They read things that neither inform or inspire them.
- They have too much fun, too often.
- They spend hours with people who cannot stimulate them.
- They read every word of advertising circulars.
- They pause to explain why they did what they did, when they should be working on the next thing.
- They hurry to the movies when they should be going to night school.
- They daydream at work when they should be planning ahead for their job.
- They spend time and energy on things that don't count.

Sound a bit harsh? No one can probably meet these standards all day every day. They are worthy guidelines, however, when we get caught in the activity trap. No one feels like being productive every day. But a bit more focus might result in substantial fulfillment.

Forget your excuses, lack of energy, aches and pains, and obsession with being busy. Do the things you know you have to do to achieve the results you want to achieve, and become the person you want to be.

A fellow doesn't last long on what he has done. He's got to keep on delivering as he goes along.
CARL
HUBBELL

TAP INTO YOUR TALENT

*If a man has talent and cannot use it, he
has failed. If he has a talent and uses only half
of it, he has partly failed. If he has
a talent and learns somehow to use the
whole of it, he has gloriously succeeded
and won satisfaction and a triumph few
men and women ever know.*

THOMAS WOLFE

FOCUS ON
WHAT YOU DO BEST

An agency rep was presented the challenge of coming up with a campaign to boost the sales of a popular laundry soap. The product had enjoyed strong customer approval for many years. What more could be said that hadn't already been discovered by users?

One day he poured a box of the soap on the top of his desk, hoping to discover something that would prompt his creativity. Suddenly, he noticed the soap was full of little blue crystals. He immediately went to the manufacturer to find out what the blue crystals were all about. What he learned sparked a successful campaign, significantly increasing sales. The blue crystals supplied the soap with super-whitening, brightening agents that made the soap so effective.

Maybe you remember the ad pitch: "Try Tide—With the New Blue Crystals." Even though the crystals had always been there, it wasn't until their purpose and effectiveness was exposed that Tide received recognition for its super-cleaning powers.

Talent without discipline is like an octopus on roller skates. There's plenty of movement, but you never know if it's going to be forward, backwards, or sideways.

H. JACKSON BROWN

I work with people every day who are like Tide. Contained inside of them is an important element whose unique value has not been exposed. They are good at what they do, but if they ever realize the latent abilities waiting to be discovered, significant achievements await them. There are gifts waiting to be opened and used.

Excellence is touched when gifts are discovered, activated, and continually repeated. How else can we explain the repeated achievements of basketball great Michael Jordan, country music star Garth Brooks, homerun king Mark McGwire, best-selling novelist Tom Clancy, actor Robin Williams, golfers Jack Nicklaus or Tiger Woods, talk-show host Oprah Winfrey, or a host of other less-renown successful people? Achievers have learned to identify, appreciate, and develop their talents by seeking opportunities to use them. Their efforts are concentrated on practicing, enjoying, and refining the gifts they have discovered.

What does this mean for common, everyday people like us? Everyone is created with the equal ability to become an unequal. Although we're not all created equal, each of us possesses the capacity to stand out from the crowd in some area of our life. One of the basic elements of success is to be good at what you do. You won't be good at what you do unless you polish your skills and perfect your moves. Master the talents you possess. Be determined to live as a "will be," not a "has been."

On Tuesday, April 18, 1995, sports fans around the country had to be a bit saddened to watch superstar Joe Montana retire from professional football after 16 seasons. Twenty thousand fans gathered in downtown San Francisco for the retirement ceremonies.

Sportscasters, coaches, and players offered their accolades to one of the league's greatest quarterbacks. However, it wasn't always like this. When Joe Montana was recruited as a third-round draft pick out of Notre Dame, San Francisco fans were less than impressed. Montana was labeled with a variety of unflattering labels.

In an answer to his critics, Joe Montana entered the league and quickly began throwing passes with perfect timing. He redefined the two-minute drill. To those who said he was too weak and scrawny to play in the big leagues, he endured season after season of physical abuse. Then, he simply went on to lead the 49'ers to four Super Bowls and helped them become a feared and dominant team in the 1980s.

Identify what's holding you back from being great. Then go out and work on turning your weaknesses into strengths.

TERRY
BRADSHAW

❧

Joe Montana will never be considered a "has been" because of his deliberate commitment to be what he "could be." Montana initially impressed very few people, but his consistent commitment to focus on what he could do best landed him in the record books and earned him the respect of the fans.

Johann Wolfgang von Goethe once said, "The man who is born with a talent which he has meant to use finds his greatest happiness in using it." To experience ongoing happiness and success with your career, find that talent that brings you joy and fulfillment.

You might say that a peak performer is a person exploring the farther reaches of his or her abilities. Push yourself to develop your talent beyond any level you may have achieved in the past.

ACHIEVEMENT HAS
NO FINISH LINE

chievers possess a dedication to action that
continually expands their potential and increases
their value. "Our business in life," said Steward
Johnson, "is not to get ahead of others, but to get ahead of
ourselves—to break our own records, to outstrip our
yesterday by our today." Such a lifestyle requires a
commitment beyond what most people are willing to make.

John Wesley committed 64 years of his life to being an
uncommon achiever for God. He had no interest in being
better than other preachers—he just tended to the business of
being his best.

Wesley preached 42,400 sermons, averaging 15
sermons per week for 54 years. He traveled 290,000 miles
(equal to circling the globe 20 times) on foot or on horseback.
No jet services were available to whisk him across the miles.
Travel, combined with his speaking schedule, was a true test
of endurance. He was a prolific author. Wesley's works,

*Peak performers
do not see
accomplishment
as a fixed state.
One of their
most engaging
characteristics
is an infectious
talent for
moving into
the future,
generating
new challenges,
living with a
sense of work
to be done.*
CHARLES
GARFIELD

including translations, amounted to over 200 volumes. When John Wesley died, at age 88, it is said he left a worn coat, a battered hat, a humble cottage, a tattered Bible, and the Methodist Church.

Wesley never considered himself as "having arrived." New sermons, spiritually hungry people, inspired vision, and the internal drive to serve captured his energy. Although the summary of your life might seem minuscule compared with John Wesley's, what you can do is achieve a little more today than you did yesterday. Work tomorrow to exceed yesterday's expectations.

Personal achievement has no finish line. As milestones are attained, encouraging you to continue, remain cautious of the temptation to put your life in neutral. Mediocrity, boredom, and uninspired standards will ultimately creep in and infect you. The antidote for these calamities is setting your sights on new peaks to scale, challenges to confront, or opportunities to master. Press on.

Set higher standards for achievement than anyone else around you. Compete with yourself to attain higher levels of performance. Unless you undertake more than you can possibly do, you will never do all you can do. This is a critical step to ongoing self-improvement that will jump-start your attitude and increase results. Self-directed pressure keeps you excited, energetic, and eager to attain heightened levels of performance.

Thomas Edison once said, "Three great essentials to achieve anything worthwhile are, first, hard work; second, stick-to-itiveness; third, common sense." I think I've adequately addressed hard work. It is summed up beautifully by James Allen: "He who would accomplish little must sacrifice little; he who would achieve much must sacrifice much."

What about stick-to-itiveness? George Bernard Shaw waited nine long years before he got anything published. Editors kept turning down everything he submitted. Undaunted by rejection, Shaw persistently kept working, writing, submitting, believing, and hoping. He also kept getting better at writing and, ultimately, got something published.

Zig Ziglar, commenting on Shaw's experience, had this observation: "Several factors are important. . . . Shaw believed that he had ability. He patiently persisted in honing his skills and pursuing publishers until finally somebody said yes. That's a good procedure to follow. If you really believe in what you're doing and have confidence that it is significant, you persist until something positive happens, knowing that it's always darkest just before the dawn."

It's easy to get fired up about a dream or goal for a short period of time. Sustaining passion in the face of adversity, rejection, or failure is the stuff of which achievers are made. Studies indicate that the one quality all successful people have is persistence. Joyce Brothers sees successful people as ". . . willing to spend more time accomplishing a task and to persevere in the face of many difficult odds. There's a very positive relationship between people's ability to accomplish any task and the time they're willing to spend on it." The power to press on in spite of everything, the power to endure—this is the achiever's quality. Persistency is the ability to face defeat, challenges, and disappointments again and again without giving up—to push on, knowing that you can attain your dreams, or at least a portion of them. Be willing to take the pains to overcome every obstacle, and to do whatever it takes.

The most vivid regrets in my life are those times when I quit too soon. A perceived lack of confidence, energy, or talent caused me to give up without realizing the fulfillment of a plan. I've since realized that any fulfillment worth its salt requires me to do the tough stuff first and realize satisfaction or reward down the road. Even when the odds are stacked against me, I've learned to overcome them by sustaining the best effort I know how.

Hang in there! Make stick-to-itiveness your ally.

I hesitate to bring up Edison's recommendation for common sense, as I don't think it can be taught. It is attained only through the practical lessons learned by everyday living. People who glean information from their life experiences and are capable of applying those lessons the next time they encounter similar situations, refine their sense of what works and what doesn't.

My advice is to thoughtfully progress along the road to your ultimate goals. Hastiness, reckless pursuit, ignoring yield and stop signs, and illogical turns rarely pay off. Stay the course. Make decisions based on the experiences you've endured.

Achievement may have no finish line, but achievers cross the line of short-term reward into a lifestyle of challenge and gratification. Every day recharges their spirit and catapults them into new ventures to enjoy.

DIG A LITTLE DEEPER

The time was the Great Depression. The place was a sheep ranch in Texas. Owner, Mr. Yates, was having severe financial difficulties and on the brink of bankruptcy. Then an oil company, believing there might be oil on his land, asked for permission to drill.

Desperate, and feeling he had nothing to lose, Mr. Yates agreed to their request. A short time later, just below the surface, the oil drillers discovered the largest oil deposit found at that time on the North American continent. Overnight, Mr. Yate's financial difficulties disappeared. He was a billionaire.

The amazing thing about this account is that the untapped wealth was there all along. He just didn't realize it.

Now, let's take this illustration a bit further. Alfred Armand Montapert, writing in *The Superior Philosophy of Man,* offered additional insight. He wrote: "In Texas, years ago, almost all of the oil came from surface operations. Then

Few people during their lifetime come anywhere near exhausting the resources dwelling within them. There are deep wells of strength that are never used.

REAR ADMIRAL RICHARD BYRD

someone got the idea that there were greater sources of supply deeper down. A well was drilled five thousand feet deep. The result? A gusher. Too many of us operate on the surface. We never go deep enough to find the supernatural resources. The result is, we never operate at our best. More time and investment is (*sic*) involved to go deep but a gusher will pay off."

How deep have you dug? How long have you been dependent on surface abilities and talents? Have you tapped your inner supply of energy and potential? Are you satisfied with being an underachiever rather than being committed to maximum achieving? Have you become complacent, doing the same things, in the same way, with the same people, every day? In other words, are you going to get any better, or is this as good as it gets?

Successful and unsuccessful people do not vary significantly in what they are capable of doing. There is a giant chasm between successful and unsuccessful people in their desire to stretch and reach toward their potential. Brian Tracy believes, "Your remarkable and unusual combination of education, experience, knowledge, problems, successes, difficulties, and challenges, and your way of looking at and reacting to life, make you extraordinary. You have within you potential competencies and attributes that can enable you to accomplish virtually anything you want in life. Your main job is to decide which of your talents you're going to exploit and develop to their highest and best possible use right now."

DIGGING DEEPER DEVICES

1. Think at a higher level. Og Mandino observed, "Your only limitations are those you set up in your mind, or permit others to set up for you." Norman Vincent Peale believed, "You are greater than you think you are."

Digging deep toward your inner potential means expanding your mental boundaries. If you keep plowing around what appears to be mental obstacles, you'll never discover potential wealth below the surface. Think beyond present constraints. You must learn to see what isn't immediately evident. Don't limit your capabilities by what you currently see. Give yourself permission to dig to the next level. What you discover will determine what gets accomplished. Each time you determine, in the privacy of your mind, to cast aside limitations, your capacity to grow and perform dramatically expands.

THE SIMPLE SECRETS of HAPPINESS

Bible scholar C.I. Scofield reflected on a visit he made to a psychiatric hospital in Staunton, Virginia. The tour guide pointed out a powerfully built young man who seemed to be a picture of health.

Scofield asked, "Wouldn't that man be very difficult to manage if he became violent?" "Yes," said the guide, "but he never exerts his power. His delusion is that he has no strength! He is always asking for medicine and complaining of weakness."

The person you think you are is the person you will be.

2. Perform at a higher level. My hunting enthusiast friends tell me there is much to learn from ducks. There are two kinds of ducks: puddle ducks and divers. Puddle ducks such as Mallards, Redheads, and Mud Hens find pleasure in paddling around the edges of ponds, marshes, and lakes. They feed in shallow waters and eat only what they can reach from the surface. Diver ducks, on the other hand, are able to dive to incredible depths in a lake to feed from the plants at the bottom. Mergansers and Canvasbacks are representative of this group. Some divers can go to depths of 150 feet for their food.

Listening to my hunter friends talk of puddle ducks and divers reminded me of a direct correlation to the different types of people. There are people who are consistently satisfied with experiences, achievements, and nourishment found in easy tasks and just being good enough at what they do. Diver people go out on a limb. They look for adventurous opportunities to test their limits and pursue situations that will not only tap but enhance their potential.

Sounds simple, doesn't it? Becoming the best you can be means continually raising the performance bar. Rather than working within a restricting zone of comfort, a concentrated effort is needed to rise above your present level of performance. Demand more of yourself. Push yourself to perform beyond the obvious minimal expectations.

What do you currently do well? How frequently are you doing it? Are you getting better at it? How can you get more out of yourself? How deep are you diving within yourself to explore and experience new-found personal resources?

3. Position yourself for a deep dig. Psychologist Abraham Maslow determined that optimal mental health had seven requirements: (1) Take responsibility for your own feelings, including your own happiness; (2) Give up the luxury of blaming others for your shortcomings, disappointments, and suffering; (3) Face the consequences, even when the things you attempt and the risks you take bring about the worst possible results; (4) Seek to discover all the inner resources that are available to you, even though self-discovery is at times painful and demanding; (5) Act on your own feelings, rather than on the approval of others—even if this means conflict at times with those who are important to you; (6) Take responsibility for letting go of your own negativity, including letting yourself and other people off the hook; and (7) Have compassion and empathy for yourself and for others, recognizing that having compassion is a very healing process.

Maslow's mental health prerequisites set you up for optimal performance. They eliminate boundaries and excuses, putting you in the driver's seat to capitalize on possibilities.

No matter how you define success, regardless of how proud you are of your achievement, you have only discovered a minute portion of all you are capable of doing. You've barely scratched the surface and owe it to yourself to dig a little deeper. You can attain a different level of success. You certainly need not settle for the way things are. There is more in you than what you've already accomplished.

Look for, plan, expect, and act to create a breakthrough experience. "Knowing is not enough, we must apply. Willing is not enough, we must do," wrote the German philosopher Goethe. Far too few people act on their dreams, goals, and ambitions, and therefore restrict ongoing success. The more you activate the digging devices, the more results you'll discover.

At the height of her acting success, Barbra Streisand decided to produce and direct the movie *Yentl*. "Why on earth would you do such a thing," friends asked her. "It had nothing to do with the desire for fame and fortune," she responded. "I had all that. I did it because one night I dreamt that I had died, and God revealed my true potential to me. He told me about all the things I could have done, but didn't because I was afraid. That was when I decided that I had to create *Yentl* even if it cost me everything I had."

Streisand decided to dig a little deeper. So can you.

He who would learn to fly one day must first learn to stand and walk and run and climb and dance; one cannot fly into flying.

FRIEDRICH W. NIETZSCHE

THE ANCHOR
OF ATTITUDE

*Real optimism is aware of problems but
recognizes the solutions, knows about
difficulties but believes they can be
overcome, sees the negatives but
accentuates the positives, is exposed
to the worst but expects the best, has
reason to complain but chooses to smile.*

WILLIAM ARTHUR WARD

MAKE EVERY HOUR
A HAPPY HOUR

Have you ever been around people who are members of the Ain't-Life-Awful club? They are such a joy with which to associate! Their conversations consist of complaining about what a cruel world we live in, gossiping about the inadequacies of others, voicing how unappreciated they feel, and sharing how the circumstances in their life are unfair. Club members are even known to leave work at the end of the day and gather for "happy hour" from 5:00–7:00 to discuss how unhappy they are.

There is only one thing worse than being around people like this: It's *being* one of those people.

"Attitude is the first quality that marks the successful man," Lowell Peacock suggested. "If he has a positive attitude and is a positive thinker, who likes challenges and difficult situations, then he has half his success achieved." Your attitude, the way you see your world, determines the way you live, and your actions determine your accomplishment. Simply put, who you are today is a result of your attitude.

The winner's edge is not in a gifted birth, a high IQ, or in talent. The winner's edge is all in the attitude, not aptitude. Attitude is the criterion for success.

DENIS WAITLEY

In his book *The Winning Attitude,* author and speaker John C. Maxwell says that attitude:

- is the "advance man" of our true selves
- has inward roots but outward fruits
- is our best friend or our worst enemy
- is more honest and more consistent than our words
- is an outward look based on past experiences
- is a thing which draws people to us or repels them
- is never content until it is expressed
- is the librarian of our past
- is the speaker of our present
- is the prophet of our future

Attitude may not be the only variable that determines your level of success, but it is certainly a primary contributor. One of the most significant attitudinal factors affecting your life is your expectation of life. Norman Vincent Peale preached, "The person who sends out positive thoughts activates the world around him positively and draws back to himself positive results."

You can learn to be more positive. There is no need to be saddled with the disheartening, deflating habit of seeing the dark side of life. If you're interested in creating an ongoing "happy hour," be assured there is only one person who can make it happen.

Begin by blocking out negativity. Stop yourself when you begin moaning, groaning, or complaining. Condition yourself to always search for the bright side of every situation. Run like crazy from negative, energy-draining people. Befriend co-workers who encourage others and display a spirit of gratitude. Focus on the present. Let go of past failures. Calm your anxiety about the future by expecting the best of today.

Before you can achieve the life you want, you must think, act, walk, talk, and behave in a way that exemplifies who you want to become. Don't expect an immediate transformation. Be patient with yourself. Lifestyle changes take time, but the result is worth the effort and wait.

DO WHAT YOU LOVE AND SUCCESS WILL FOLLOW

The talent of success is nothing more than doing what you can do well; and doing well whatever you do, without the thought of fame.

HENRY
WADSWORTH
LONGFELLOW

❋

I've had the opportunity to encounter and observe a few people, who have quietly attained success without the fanfare or recognition of a fan club or fame. As I've watched their daily behavior, it has become evident that success is the result of the continual process of them becoming who they already were and loving what they do. No pretenses, no uncharacteristic behaviors, no facades; just a revealing of true character.

A fundamental characteristic of successful people is their ability to find out what they are good at and do it with a passion regardless of whether or not anyone else notices. Curtis Carlson advises, "You must listen to your own heart. You can't be successful if you aren't happy with what you're doing." The key here is being involved in something that utilizes your natural abilities. I can think of nothing worse than attempting to motivate myself in a position or activity that does not compliment my talents.

Michael Korda said, "Your chances of success are directly proportional to the degree of pleasure you derive from what you do. If you are in a job you hate, face the fact squarely and get out." As the old saying goes, "If the horse is dead, dismount." I don't think it's possible to ascend any further than what you are without first making sure that where you are is where you want to be.

Before jumping overboard, however, consider this. If you have a job that fails to stimulate, fulfill, and energize you, maybe there is a simple solution. How about changing your attitude about your job? Maybe you don't have to dismount. Could it be possible that changing how you view your life could ignite a new flame?

Whit Hobbs wrote, "Success is waking up in the morning, whoever you are, wherever you are, however old or young, and bounding out of bed because there's something out there that you love to do, that you believe in, that you're good at—something that's bigger than you are, and you can hardly wait to get at it again today."

Approaching everything you do with that upbeat attitude is bound to result in success.

Career is too pompous a word. It was a job, and I have always felt privileged to be paid for what I am doing.

BARBARA STANWYCK

CAREER-GUIDING PRINCIPLES

You pay a price for getting stronger. You pay a price for getting faster. You pay a price for jumping higher. (But also) you pay a price for staying just the same.

H. JACKSON BROWN

Life's Little Instruction Book

❀

If you were to leave your job today, what legacy would you leave? St. Augustine once said that adulthood begins when a person asks himself the question, "What do I want to be remembered for?" Have you begun your adulthood? Do you have any idea what affect you are making on those around you? Are there certain character traits, actions, or idiosyncrasies that will immediately make people think of you?

An unknown writer once communicated, "Methods are many; principles are few. Methods always change; principles never do." Principles are heart issues. It's difficult to communicate in written word the emotion that ignites these motivating forces. Nevertheless, here are the unchangeable principles that have guided, formed, and directed my life the past 20 years.

1. My attitude about life will determine my quality of life. Circumstances rarely dictate performance, but my perception of those events has dramatically affected my ability to deal with them. I figure there are two ways of approaching life: Either alter the circumstances, or alter yourself to meet them. What really matters is not the way things are, but the way you think things are, and how you decide to respond. John Maxwell is convinced that, "What I believe about life determines how I perceive life, which determines what I receive from life."

Your perception of and reaction to life's events will determine the affect they have on you. Every incident is merely an event waiting for you to develop an opinion about it. The attitude I display in life is a reflection of my internal beliefs, assumptions, and values. "You and I do not see things as they are," says Herb Cohen. "We see things as we are."

This is more than positive thinking. It is a process of making a conscious decision about what you will dwell on and how you will interpret any given situation.

2. There is a miniscule difference between success and failure. Success begins on the inside. NBA legend Michael Jordan said, "Heart is what separates the good from the great." Newsman Walter Cronkite declared, "I can't imagine a person becoming a success who doesn't give this game of life everything he's got."

The late Billy Martin was a controversial manager for the New York Yankees and established nonnegotiable standards for his players to follow. He let players know in no uncertain terms, "If you play for me, you play the game like you play life. You play it to be successful, you play it with dignity, you play it with pride, you play it aggressively, and you play it as well as you possibly can."

Are you getting the picture here? Successful people do a little more, raise the performance bar a little higher, expect higher results, and stick it out when things aren't going exactly as planned. Successful people invest 110 percent of themselves in their relationships. They continually monitor their attitude and make sure their energies are directed at their top priorities. They understand the need for total commitment to the task at hand and are determined to see it through to successful completion. Successful people are involved in a lifelong process of skill and competency development. They're not afraid to stand out from the crowd. In fact, they rather enjoy it.

Successful people do what's expected . . . and a little bit more. After Dallas won the Super Bowl in 1993, coach Jimmy Johnson commented, "I played for a national championship team, I coached a national championship team, and I coached a Super Bowl team. There's a common thread in all three: quality people who are committed to do their best." It's the miniscule difference between success and failure.

3. Personal growth precedes personal fulfillment. Bruce Springsteen believes, "A time comes when you need to stop waiting for the man you want to become and start being the man you want to be." You will never become what you ought to be until you begin doing what you ought to be doing to become what you want to be. Feeling good about your life is preceded by a willingness to learn, grow, and produce beyond your current accomplishments.

Sad is the day when people become content with their life, what they think, and the results they are producing. A multitude of opportunities await us every day to expand. Failure to pursue those windows of possibility will leave us unfulfilled and dissatisfied with life. It's not life's fault. Revitalize your life with a renewed commitment to a dream, results, and desire to tap into your potential achievement.

"If you're not doing something with your life," began a Peace Corps commercial, "it doesn't matter how long it is."

Life becomes boring when you stop growing and stretching. You become boring.

4. When I help others to be successful, I will be successful. The most successful people in the world are those who help other people become better and achieve more than they ever thought they could. Alan Lay McGinnis put it this way: "There is no more noble occupation in the world than to assist another human being—to help someone succeed."

I'm often asked what I mean by "helping someone succeed." Accept people with all of their irritating habits and idiosyncrasies—you have them, too. Always expect and discover the best in people. Listen without judgment and look them in the eye when they are talking. Pray for people. Share your affection. Laugh with people and cry with them as well. Send notes of encouragement and appreciation. Refrain from jealousy and anger. Celebrate people's successes with them. Go out of your way to be kind. Eliminate all ill will. Learn what is important to people and stand side by side with them in achieving their goals. Be a stimulant. Get excited about other people's lives and make it a point to help every person you work, live, or socialize with to feel important.

Joann C. Jones, writing in *Guideposts,* relayed the following story. "During my second year of nursing school our professor gave us a pop quiz. I breezed through the questions until I read the last one: 'What is the first name of the woman who cleans the school?'

"Surely this was some kind of joke. I had seen the cleaning woman several times, but how would I know her name? I handed in my paper, leaving the last question blank.

"Before the class ended, one student asked if the last question would count toward the grade. 'Absolutely,' the professor said. 'In your careers you will meet many people. All are significant. They deserve your attention and care, even if all you do is smile and say hello.'

"I've never forgotten that lesson. I also learned her name was Dorothy."

Helping others succeed is a simple, yet profound process of continually finding ways to enrich people's lives. From simply knowing their name, to walking step by step, side by side toward their dreams, your life will be filled with a multitude of moments to make a difference.

5. Walk the talk. St. Francis of Assisi once wisely said: "Preach the gospel at all times. If necessary, use words." We get so busy in the activities of life, we forget above all else what our life is communicating to others. Personality, work ethic, achievements, and our interactions with people display our good intentions. Who we are is the message. "So live that you wouldn't be ashamed to sell the family parrot to the town gossip," advised Will Rogers.

In his book with Ken Blanchard, *Everyone's a Coach,* Don Shula tells of losing his temper near an open microphone during a televised game with the Los Angeles Rams. Millions of viewers expressed surprise and shock by Shula's profanity. Letters arrived from all over the country, voicing their dissatisfaction and disbelief that this man of integrity could display such behavior.

Shula could have been tempted to offer excuses, but he didn't. Everyone who included a return address received a personal apology. He closed each letter by stating, "I value your respect and will do my best to earn it again."

Walking the talk doesn't mean living without mistakes but it does mean you are accountable for your behavior. Zig Ziglar was right. "Integrity," he says, "demands that you do the right thing so that you have fewer things to apologize for, explain away, or regret. Instead, cut your losses as quickly as possible after making a poor decision." Be quick to apologize when you fail to live up to the standards for which you hold yourself accountable.

Mark Twain knew how difficult it was to live an exemplary life. He once observed, "To do right is wonderful. To teach others to do right is even more wonderful—and much easier."

6. Take responsibility for your life. Never allow someone else or something outside of your control prevent you from succeeding. Give up all excuses, the blame game, and finger-pointing. "Success on any major scale requires you to accept responsibility," advises Michael Korda, editor-in-chief of Simon & Schuster. "In the final analysis, the one quality that all successful people have is the ability to take on responsibility."

You are completely responsible for what you do. Bern Williams has identified our modern-day unwillingness to take responsibility by speculating, "If Adam and Eve were alive today, they would probably sue the snake." We might chuckle at his suggestion, but I fear it is closer to the truth than most of us care to admit.

Responsibility is dreaded by many, but it is one choice that will make a substantial difference in changing your life. If you want to be happy with the life you live, get in charge. Take responsibility for where you are and where you're going. You are accountable for the results. You always have been and always will be. That's probably why Ed Cole suggested, "Maturity doesn't come with age; it comes with acceptance of responsibility."

Here's why this principle is so important. If you don't accept responsibility, you will soon identify yourself as a victim, and victims lead lives full of frustration, rationalization, blame, defensiveness, and excuses. I've cherished two questions that guard me from the snare of victimization. First, what do I want? Second, what am I willing to do to make it happen? The responsibility is on one person—me.

7. Be willing to pay the price. I've observed two kinds of people: those who get things done and those who wait for all the conditions to be just right before attempting anything. There are those who do whatever it takes and those who continually protest, "That's not my job." Zig Ziglar recommends, "If you do the things you need to do when you need to do them, the day will come when you can do the things you want to do when you want to do them."

Achievement is the result of doing what needs to be done, whether or not you feel like doing them. Don't wait to feel good before doing good. Pay the price now and experience the satisfaction of defying those little voices that tell you you're just not up to the task right now. "To achieve success, whatever the job we have, we must pay a price for success," said Vince Lombardi. "You have to pay the price to win and you have to pay the price to get to the point where success is possible. Most important, you must pay the price to stay there."

Legendary UCLA basketball coach John Wooden epitomized this principle. He never took success for granted. He knew there was a price to be paid each year, and resting on last year's success was not acceptable. He prepared his teams for battle. The continual development of skills, attitudes, teamwork, and a championship mindset produced phenomenal results. Wooden was so focused that he even required players to put on their socks a certain way, replace the soap in the shower stalls, and stack their dirty towels.

Ironically, as meticulous as Wooden was, he never relied on scouting reports or playbooks. He didn't want his players worrying about the opponent's weaknesses or strengths. He found playbooks useless because in the heat of the game, he knew he would need to make adjustments that couldn't be precalculated or written into a book of standard plays.

When you pay the price day in and day out, no matter how tedious or demanding it might seem, you will be rewarded with a champion lifestyle.

8. Live to give. "The measure of a life, after all, is not its duration but its donation," said Corrie Ten Boom. Generosity is a marvelous quality.

In our society, money tends to be the measuring stick for giving. What was her salary increase last year? How big was his performance bonus? What did that new car cost him? What was the increase in the bottom line? Our culture is obsessed with what people get.

Living to give involves so much more. The grave of Christopher Chapman in Westminster Abbey, bearing the date 1680, reads: *What I gave, I have; What I spent, I had; What I left, I lost; By not giving it.*

It's difficult to convince selfish people to begin giving of their resources, time, and talent. Sometimes it's easiest to write a check and hope nothing more is required. Step out by sharing thoughtfulness, sensitivity, and kindness with those needing a bit of compassion. Never turn your head on a co-worker needing to feel included.

Help someone who cannot help you in return. Encourage those who cannot help themselves. Nurture someone in moving toward his or her potential. Create a generous heart and heaven will be filled with people cheering when you get there.

9. Live every day to the fullest. "If you let yourself be absorbed completely," suggested Anne Morrow Lindbergh, "if you surrender completely to the moments as they pass, you live more richly in those moments."

This is such a simple principle for living, I am almost embarrassed to include it in the list. Yet, it seems people are always preparing to live. Someday they'll enjoy their job. Someday they'll have time for those they love. Someday they'll get actively involved in the adventure of living. What are they waiting for? Someday may never come.

Life isn't a dress rehearsal for the main event. You are living the main event. Look at your calendar for the week. Are there appointments, things on your to-do list, or responsibilities you dread? Decide you will meet them with a renewed passion. Look for little blessings in every corner of your life. Capture the miracle of life by giving each moment you live your best. Live every minute of every day to the fullest. Who knows, it might be your last.

"Seize the moment," encouraged Erma Bombeck. "Remember all those women on the *Titanic* who waved off the dessert cart."

10. Keep success in perspective. Singer Jon Bon Jovi's parents told him he could achieve anything, so he worked tirelessly on his musical career from the time he was 16. His band became phenomenally successful, but Jon Bon Jovi hit the wall and realized there had to be more to life than the reckless pace, physical exhaustion, or continual pressure to produce another No. 1 album or No. 1 single. His wife, Dorothea, gave him the room and encouragement to put it all in perspective.

"Today," says Bon Jovi, "I try to spend as much time on my marriage and parenting as I do on my career. For years we had a funny adage in our house that was, 'It's about me, me, me, the singer.' Now it's no longer about me, it's about them. We stay home, making sure the kids have a healthy, loving environment."

Success is all about recognizing and appreciating the love and respect of those closest to you. What good is success if the people around you are being hurt in the process? What good is success if it is not contributing to the long-term health and benefit of those you love? What good is success if you don't have someone you love to share it with?

As much as I enjoy the pursuit of dreams, goals, and accomplishments, the long-term value is small compared with the privilege of savoring each day with those I love and respect.

That's it. The ten principles that guide my life are simple, but they've been effective in providing a compass for my personal and professional pursuits. How about you? Have you decided what unwavering, unchangeable principles will direct your life?

BUILD A
BETTER YOU

Character is what we do when no one is
looking. It is not the same as reputation . . .
success . . . achievement. Character is not
what we have done, but who we are.

BILL HYBELS

PAY ATTENTION TO
WHO YOU ARE

John Luther once said, "Good character is more to be praised than outstanding talent. Most talents are, to some extent, a gift. Good character, by contrast, is not given to us. We have to build it piece by piece—by thought, choice, courage, and determination." Character has to do with how people are put together. It's the interaction between what they believe and what they do. Although talent is important to be successful in your job, character is imperative.

In his book *Everything You've Heard Is Wrong,* Tony Campolo tells this great story. Once upon a time there was an office manager who lost his job during the recession. In his sadness he wandered into a park, found himself an empty bench, and sat down. After a while another man came strolling along. This second man was especially sad as he took a seat at the opposite end of the bench.

Hard work spotlights the character of people: some turn up their sleeves, some turn up their noses, and some don't turn up at all.

SAM EWING

After these two men had sat silently for a couple of hours, the first man said, "I'm an office manager who has been made redundant. I don't have a job anymore. What's your problem?"

The second man answered, "I own a circus. The big attraction at my circus was an ape. Last week the ape died, and the crowds have fallen off to almost nothing. I think I'm going to be out of business if I don't find another ape."

It did not take long for the first man to come up with an interesting proposal. "You need an ape and I need a job. What if I dress up in the ape's skin and pretend to be real? I could carry on for your patrons and everybody would be happy."

Having nothing to lose, the circus owner decided to give it a try. To his surprise the fake ape proved to be more exciting and drew larger crowds than the real one had. Money came pouring in, and both the former office manager and the circus owner were getting rich.

Then, one day, things got out of hand. Somehow a lion got into the same cage with the fake ape. The office manager didn't know what to do. He maneuvered as best he could to escape the claws of the lion but realized that sooner or later he would be a "goner."

A large crowd gathered outside the cage to watch the spectacle. They screamed and gasped as the lion finally trapped the office manager in a corner of the cage and poised himself to leap on the make-believe ape. Suddenly, the shocked crowd heard the ape yell in a shaken, frightened voice, "Help! Help!"

It was then that the lion muttered under his breath, "Shut up, stupid! Do you think you're the only one around here that's out of a job?"

It's amazing how many people are walking around pretending to be something they aren't. They invest substantial energy creating an identity that will be acceptable to those around them. The problem is, they find it necessary to keep changing their public appearance to meet the vacillating expectations of the people they are with. It's impossible to play this game for a lifetime. Sooner or later, they get cornered and the "real person" is exposed.

Career success is grounded in behavior that is consistent with the values we espouse. Violating personal values is harmful to the person as well as the organization. Pretending leads to personal sabotage and self-protective behaviors. I would have to agree with John Morley, who observed, "No man can climb out beyond the limitations of his own character." When your character is strong, people trust you to perform up to your potential. When character is questionable, people never know what to expect.

Be a professional who knows what's right and does it, even if it means putting forth substantially more effort. Doing what's easy or convenient isn't necessarily consistent with what's right.

Let your commitment to values drive your actions. Is it risk free? Will it be well received? Am I in the mood to do it? These are not the questions values-driven people ask. Are my behaviors in line with my ethical commitment? Do I believe in what I'm doing? Am I maintaining my integrity with this decision? These are the questions that surface when character is in charge.

Maintain the highest standards. Your character comes to life through your values, integrity, and honesty . . . the consistency between your words and actions. Understand that your convictions might not initially win a popularity contest, especially if they violate "the way we've always done it." Remind yourself that the right things are not always rewarded and not everybody will be on your side.

Take full responsibility for your character. "Everybody's doing it" is juvenile and doesn't cut it. You can't put someone else in charge of your ethics. Try it, and you'll soon find yourself lowering your standards. "I'm just doing what I'm told" is a cop out. Character is a personal decision and quest. Your beliefs might coincide with the people you work with, but ultimately character is an individual exercise.

Character-driven people are willing to do the things emotion-driven people will not do. They take pride in their dependability, commitment to excellence, willingness to serve others, solution-minded approach to problems and their internal drive . . . regardless of how they "feel." This isn't a sometime thing or a 90-percent thing; either you have it or you don't. Even brief leaks can be devastating.

According to a 1997 *USA Today* article, scientists are now convinced that a series of slits, not a gash, sank the *Titanic*.

As the extremely successful movie reminded us, the 900-foot unsinkable cruise ship sank in 1912 on its first voyage, from England to New York. Fifteen hundred people met a tragic death in this ocean disaster.

The widely held belief that the ship hit an iceberg, resulting in a huge gash in the side of the liner, is now in question. An international team of divers and scientists used sound waves to probe the wreckage, resting in mud two-and-a-half miles deep. They were shocked to find the damage to the ship was relatively small. Instead of a huge gash, they discovered six relatively narrow slits across the six water-tight holds.

What an incredible find! Six small leaks caused the demise of a giant, steel vessel. Likewise, small leaks, insignificant compromises, undefined parameters, and ignored values can sink a person's character. Pay attention to who you are. It's more than a reputation. Reputation is what you are supposed to be. Character is what you are.

Like the *Titanic,* a reputation doesn't mean much unless it can stand up under a lifetime of pressure. Be encouraged by the words of Bobby Richardson who said, "Any man will command respect if he takes a stand and backs it up with his life."

GET A BETTER VIEW
OF YOURSELF

Doubt yourself and you doubt everything you see. Judge yourself and you see judges everywhere. But if you listen to the sound of your own voice, you can rise above doubt and judgment, and you can see forever.

NANCY
KERRIGAN

❋

rom *Sunday Sermons* comes the story of a man who brought his boss home for dinner for the first time. The boss was very blustery, very arrogant, very dominating! The little boy in the family stared at his father's boss for most of the evening, but did not say anything. Finally, the boss asked the little boy, "Why do you keep looking at me like that, Sonny?" The little boy answered, "My daddy says you are a self-made man." The boss beamed and proudly admitted that indeed he was a self-made man. The little boy said, "Well, if you are a self-made man, why did you make yourself like that?"

This little story prompts a chuckle every time I think about it. The little boy's comment also creates a few sobering thoughts. We all have our own struggles with becoming the person we want to be. There may be times we even ask ourselves: "Why did I make myself like this?"

During one of my seminars, I often ask the question, "How many of you believe in yourself 100 percent?" Rarely does a hand go up. As I work my way down the percentage scale, the majority of hands are raised somewhere between 50 and 75 percent. Two important questions are then posed to the group: (1) What keeps you from achieving 100 percent, and (2) What would your work place be like if everyone believed in themselves 100 percent?

Believing in yourself 100 percent does not equate with arrogance, pride, or conceit. It's the maximum utilization of the gifts, abilities, and talents you've been given. On the flip side, believing in yourself halfway will not provide the motivation necessary to go beyond where you are.

Much of our insecurity about ourselves on the job is prompted by feeling we're not so good as other people and there's little chance things are going to get any better. To break out of this thinking, we need to reform our current beliefs and begin questioning the assumptions we make about ourselves.

Breaking through cemented images we have of ourselves is no easy task. Begin by seeing the person you want to become and then work backwards to make that image a reality. My friend Joe Batten says, "When you know who and what we wish to be, we will find it relatively easy to know what to do." Begin acting like the person you want to become. Portray the confidence that person will have. Behave as if you are already that person. As you begin getting a better view of yourself, keep a few things in mind.

Be yourself. Brian Tracy believes, "The world will largely accept you at your own estimation. It is yourself that you have to convince before you can convince anyone else."

Willy Loman, in the powerful, yet tragic play, *Death of a Salesman,* lived a life filled with phony clichés. Willy struggled to discover who he really was and because of this lived a life of fear, doubt, and insecurity. *Death of a Salesman* recently experienced a surge in popularity. I can't help but wonder if Willy Loman is more than a character for those who attend the play. Could it be he portrays a world full of people trying to be like, act like, and succeed like other people? "So much restlessness," suggests Lin Yutang, "is due to the fact that one does not know what one wants, or wants too many things, or perhaps wants to be somebody else; to be anybody except one's self. There is courage in being one's genuine self, or standing alone and not wanting to be somebody else."

Theologian Charles Spurgeon warned, "Beware of no one more than yourself; we carry our worst enemies within us." It's important to discover who you really are—your character, values, and heart—before you attempt to build on what you have. "Human being" does indeed precede "human doing."

Be genuine. Unfortunately, Ava Gardner represented a lot of people when she said, "Deep down, I'm pretty superficial."

The best way to describe what I mean by being genuine is to share an illustration that is totally contrary to what I mean. In the October 26, 1992 issue of *The New York Times,* an article headlined "Fragrance Engineers Say They Can Bottle the Smell of Success," by N.R. Kleinfield, begins like this:

"It was bound to happen. Someone thinks he is about to create the Honest Car Salesman in a bottle.

"A year ago, one of Detroit's Big Three auto makers hired Dr. Alan R. Hirsch, a quirky smell researcher in Chicago, to devise a rather exceptional scent. The hope was that when the odor was sprayed on a car salesman, he would—yes—smell honest.

"It sounds absurd. In fact, after she was done laughing, Dr. Susan Shiffman, a smell researcher and professor of medical psychology at the Duke University Medical School, remarked, 'I was not aware that honesty had a specific smell associated with it.' But Dr. Hirsch, who refuses to name his Detroit client, is confident that he will have the Honest Car Salesman Odor devised within a year. If he succeeds, he said, the auto maker will entrust the smell to its dealers, who will spray it on their salesmen, and then customers will catch a whiff and cars will fly off the lots."

Believe it or not, this is a true story. My response is, "If you're trying to cover up a character flaw with a scented spray, don't expect to achieve a respectable reputation or increased self respect." Norman Vincent Peale once said, "It is a fact that you project what you are." Be genuine. Phonies ultimately end up disliking themselves.

Be assured you are somebody special. According to *Parade,* the 1992 November ballot in the state of Washington carried a candidate named "Absolutely Nobody." David Powers had his name legally changed to capitalize on voter frustration and promised to abolish the office of Lieutenant Governor if elected. He lost with 6 percent of the vote, but what if he had won? "Absolutely Nobody Wins!"

How true! People who believe they are nobody never win. They might get attention or even sympathy, but it's short lived and they end with a small percent of support, leaving them worse off than they were before. "My advice is, follow my advice," advises Miss Piggy. "Never forget that only you can ever fully appreciate your own true beauty. Others may try, but they so often fall short." Louis L'Amour said it a little differently, "I am somebody. I am me. I like being me. And I need nobody to make me somebody." Being somebody special begins with believing you are somebody special. See your own goodness, appreciate your assets, and celebrate your humanness.

In addition, Denis Waitley suggests, "Faith in yourself begins with understanding that God is always with you and within you." Waitley's comment is comforting. God is bigger than any limitation you possess and capable of turning your greatest weakness into a strength.

There is a story told by entertainer Roger Williams that has some relevance here. It seems the famous singer was on tour and stopped by a nursing home to visit his mother. He said he got lost looking for her room and was wandering around somewhat confused when an elderly woman came up to him and looked at him with an intensely curious, but recognizing stare. After a moment, he awkwardly broke the silence asking, "Do you know who I am?"

THE SIMPLE SECRETS of HAPPINESS

You are free to choose where you work, what you do, and with whom you will work. But who and what you become is hanging in the balance. Before you take a job or position, remind yourself that what will go on in the workplace will change you, and ask yourself whether or not the change will be in harmony with your mission statement.

TONY
CAMPOLO

Surveying him from head to toes, she replied, "No, but if you go to the front desk, they can tell you."

We don't need someone else telling us who we are, but to increase our value to the company, our co-workers and customers, knowing who we are and striving to be what we want to become is important. Dr. Joyce Brothers reminds us, "You cannot consistently perform in a manner which is inconsistent with the way you see yourself." Therefore, staying neutral is not an option. We need to move forward to discipline ourselves toward positive, constructive action that moves us continually in the direction of becoming all we can be. That's how you get a better view of yourself.

BE THE BEST YOU
CAN BE

John C. Maxwell, writing in *Developing the Leader Within You,* says, "Most people have a desire to look at the exception instead of the desire to become the exceptional." The reality is, it takes a ton of effort to become exceptional and very little effort to find excuses for why we aren't performing at our best. There is a personal price to pay to excel in your career. No shortcuts are available.

"Excellence," says Pat Riley, "is the gradual result of always striving to do better." Notice Riley didn't say, "If you do this one thing, you'll have mastered the formula for excellence." Reaching your optimum performance requires small steps to help you grow so you're prepared for your next level of performance. I've observed a number of practical strategies employed by people who realize and are motivated by the fact that "average" is as close to the bottom as it is to the top. They don't want to spend their career in that limbo position.

If you want to achieve excellence, you can get there today. As of this second, quit doing less than excellent work.

THOMAS WATSON

Different things seem to work for different people. However, a few of the strategies are relatively universal. Consider the following approaches for planning your excursion away from average toward your peak performance.

1. Fix the flaws. Running back Rashaan Salaam's outstanding rushing career in college earned him the Heisman Trophy in 1995. He was drafted by the Chicago Bears, and although he led the Bears in rushing during the rookie season, opponents spotted a weakness in his game. Salaam was prone to fumble. In fact, he gave up the ball nine times.

According to the *Chicago Tribune,* the Chicago Bears's coaching staff devised a practical drill to correct the problem. They tied a long strap around a football. As Rashaan ran with the ball tightly clutched against his body, another player ran behind him yanking on the strap. Rashaan learned to squeeze the ball with such power that it could not be forced free.

People who are committed to excellence in their careers identify what top-notch performance would look like and then move towards that standard. As this process evolves, needed corrections unfold and adjustments are made to insure a steady progress toward the ideal. Minor flaws, imperfections, and less-than-desirable outcomes are bound to surface. That's a natural part of the process. What separates the excellent from the mediocre performers is the determination to correct faults that undermine their desire to be the best they can be. As Oliver Cromwell said in the early 17th century, "The person who stops being better, stops being good." It's a never-ending quest.

I'm not an advocate for investing massive attention and energy on fixing what's wrong and letting the strengths take care of themselves. Quite the contrary. Yet, you can't overlook those issues that keep you from scaling new heights, refining your expertise, or achieving expanded results. But just removing or correcting the weaknesses doesn't mean everything will be perfect. You might have an error-free day, but not necessarily one that could be defined as excellent. Rashaan Salaam may not fumble the ball during an entire game, but that doesn't mean he has a successful day in the backfield. More is needed than "just" managing our limitations or weaknesses.

2. Find your sweet spot. After decades of work as a consultant with major companies and a prolific writing career, Peter Drucker made this observation: "The great mystery isn't that people do things badly but that they occasionally do a few things well. The only thing that is universal is incompetence. However, nobody ever comment-ed, for example, that the great violinist, Jascha Heifetz, probably couldn't play the trumpet very well."

Finding that niche, talent, or interest where excellence can be achieved is a great way to maximize your efforts. When we find that "sweet spot," as in tennis or golf, increased power and control are at our disposal.

As Alfred North Whitehead put it, "Doing little things well is the way toward doing big things better."

Capitalizing on your sweet spot keeps you reaching, stretching to perfect your skills and to outdo yesterday. You may see bit-by-bit improvement, but it's enough to eventually add up to a significant increase in your expertise. Use your sweet spots to trigger dramatic performance breakthroughs, protect your career, improve your value to the company, and prepare the way for a bright future. Think of it as a daily pursuit of perfection that will upgrade your contribution to the team and organization.

3. Focus on doing your best. While serving in the United States Navy, Jimmy Carter applied for the nuclear submarine program. Admiral Hyman Rickover was the head of the United States Nuclear Navy at the time, and everyone knew about his reputation for being a stern and demanding admiral. Jimmy Carter had to interview with the legendary admiral. Those who had endured past interviews knew that applicants usually came out in fear, anger, and totally intimidated. But, he was the door that had to be passed through.

Carter reflected that, for the first part of the interview, the admiral allowed him to talk about any topic he wanted to discuss. He chose subjects that were familiar to him, but by the time the admiral asked him increasingly difficult questions about the topic, Carter learned he knew relatively little about the subject.

Toward the end of the interview, the Admiral asked, "How did you stand in your class at the Naval Academy?" Carter proudly answered, "Sir, I stood fifty-ninth in a class of 820." He fully expected a hearty congratulations from the admiral, but instead received a surprising response. Rickover asked, "Did you do your best?"

Carter began to answer, "Yes, sir," but then took a moment to reflect on times when he could have learned more about America's allies and enemies, weapons, strategy, and the like. He finally responded, "No, sir, I didn't always do my best."

Admiral Rickover looked at Carter for a long time, turned his chair around to end the interview, and then threw one final question at his applicant. He said, "Why not?"

Was Admiral Rickover too harsh? Did he demand too much of a young seaman? Were his expectations unrealistic? Not according to Jimmy Carter. He said he never forgot Admiral Rickover's words to him that day. Years later, that encounter prompted a title for his book: *Why Not the Best?*

In an effort to keep up in this fast-paced world, some people lower their standards and expect less than excellence from themselves. Sacrifices are made in the name of efficiency. Unfortunately, such a move can reduce a person's performance to mediocrity. Colin Powell is right, "The freedom to be your best means nothing unless you're willing to do your best."

"Are you doing your best?" Raise your standards. Establish a baseline of which you can be proud. Make no exceptions. Instead of accepting less than your best, improve upon your personal best. "Aim at perfection in everything," suggested Lord Chesterfield, "though in most things, it is unattainable. However, they who aim at it, and persevere, will come much nearer to it than those whose laziness and despondency make them give it up as unattainable." Reach for new heights. Go above and beyond the call of duty. Do more than others expect. Never accept so-so performance in yourself or those around you.

This is a great time to be the best you can be . . . in everything . . . in every way.

Over and over again mediocrity is promoted because real worth isn't to be found.

KATHLEEN NORRIS

MAKE THINGS HAPPEN

Nothing is so fatiguing as the eternal hanging on of an uncompleted task.

WILLIAM JAMES

COMPLETE
UNCOMPLETED TASKS

W hat do you remember most—the tasks you have completed or those you have yet to do? Most people immediately respond, "I remember most the things I have left to do."

I'm always challenged (and often embarrassed) when I arrive home at night and my wife asks, "What did you do today?" There are some days I must honestly respond, "I don't know for sure. But it took me all day to do it."

Failure to make significant progress completing work demands is a major source of frustration, stress, and disappointment. Only an obsession for completion can erase the negative results and feelings associated with loose ends.

Existing in a frantic whirlwind of commitments and activities is not the same as producing results. In fact, an estimated one-third of the American workforce doesn't accomplish what it sets out to do each day. Is it any wonder why we have a nation of unfulfilled workers?

What you accomplish in life depends almost completely upon what you make yourself do. The very first thing one should do is to train the mind to concentrate upon the essentials and discard the frivolous and unimportant. This will assure real accomplish-ment and ultimate success.

LYNDON
JOHNSON

Henry David Thoreau observed, "It's not enough to be industrious, so are the ants. What are you industrious about?"

What is your definition of work? Is it a series of activities and responsibilities? If so, then work is viewed as a verb. Everybody works, but not everybody is productive.

Productive people see work as what they are able to achieve. It is a noun. What evolves out of completed tasks is a feeling of being in control, increased productivity, heightened satisfaction, increased time for other responsibilities, and more energy to be creative. Until we develop a mindset that what we achieve is far more important than being busy, completing uncompleted tasks will not be a priority.

Review your pending assignments, the pile of unread journal articles, correspondence awaiting your reply, and the return phone calls you've been avoiding. Simplify your approach and plan to unclutter your life (and desk) by seeing these responsibilities through to completion.

Completion produces a satisfaction that the result has been achieved. You can mark it off your to-do list and get a fresh start. There's a new freedom to pursue the next priority. Creativity increases. Your energy tank will be refilled and you will be able to refocus attention. A renewed momentum is in place.

Look for ways to bring closure and completion to your daily assignments. We live in a time when working hard is not nearly so important as getting work done. You will be recognized and remembered for what you have done, not for how busy you were or how good your intentions were.

Simple hint: If you have difficulty bringing closure to your work, pretend you're going on vacation next week. I'm convinced a national survey would produce a phenomenal correlation between efficiency, effectiveness, results, and the timing of vacations.

HALF
FINISHED

If you are
wearing out the
seat of your
pants before
you do your
shoe soles,
you're making
too many
contacts in the
wrong place.
ANONYMOUS

❋

Winter in the Midwest provides ample opportunity for any youngster with a little gumption to benefit from the lack of motivation displayed by others. After a heavy snowfall, we would grab our shovels and go in search of adults discouraged by nature's actions. Youthful ingenuity led us to people whose driveways were half finished. In fact, hearing someone say, "Can't you see I'm already half finished?" tickled our hearts. These people lost interest in their activity and would usually turn over their driveway (and their money) to our ambitions and willingness to finish what they had started.

Stick-to-itiveness is a quality lacking in the day-to-day affairs of many people. We can never be what we ought to be until we start doing what we ought to be doing. Then we need to continue doing what we ought to be doing so we can achieve what we are capable of achieving. "You will never stub your toe standing still," reflected Charles F. Kettering. "The faster you go, the more chance there is of stubbing your toe, but the more chance you have of getting somewhere."

Don't get bogged down in preparing to take action. Preparation is often a stall tactic, an excuse for fearing what your actions might produce or fail to produce. Very little can be accomplished unless you go ahead and do it before you're ready. When you hear someone constantly talking about what they are going to do tomorrow, rest assured they probably said the same thing yesterday.

A lifestyle of inactivity, procrastination, or quitting perpetuates itself. There is a cure. William James, the father of American psychology, suggested three rules for making things happen in life:

1. Start immediately.

2. Do it flamboyantly.

3. No exceptions.

Put another way, get up, get active, wear out your soles, and stick to it with unwavering tenacity. "To know what has to be done, and then do it," said Sir William Osler, "comprises the whole philosophy of practical life."

Take time to deliberate; but when the time for action arrives, stop thinking and go in.
ANDREW JACKSON

FILL HOLES OR
PLANT TREES

If you ever think you're too small to be effective, you've never been in bed with a mosquito.

ANITA RODDICK

I love the story about a farmer sitting on his porch watching a highway department work crew. A worker got out of the truck, dug a good-sized hole in the ditch, and climbed back into the vehicle. A few minutes later, a pick-up truck pulled up as the first truck drove forward on the shoulder of the road. A worker stepped out of the pick-up, filled up the hole, tamped the dirt, and got back in his vehicle. The two-man work crew repeated the process—digging, waiting, refilling. After a few repetitions, the farmer made his way to the workers. "What are you doing?" he asked.

"We're on a beautification project," one worker responded, "and the guy who plants the trees is on vacation."

I like being around people who make things happen. Organizations need people who want to make a difference, not those who simply keep busy, like the beautification crew. These "busy" people keep filling holes without creating visible improvements or generating results. Call it busy work without productivity. These people are a dime a dozen.

On the other hand, co-workers who are excited about their responsibilities, recognize the importance of their role, apply themselves to the job at hand, and desire to improve the way things are achieve appreciable results. No matter how seemingly unimportant or insignificant their role, they keep moving forward, positioning themselves to perform on a higher plane.

Organizations need people willing to take initiative by making bold moves to advance the organization's effectiveness. There's plenty of room for people who constantly think of new ways to contribute to the team. Shattering the *status quo,* endorsing risk, and making gutsy moves to benefit the organization isn't written in their job descriptions. These are the unwritten qualifications that separate mediocre and successful people. As William Arthur Ward said, "Blessed is the person who sees the need, recognizes the responsibility, and actively becomes the answer."

Watching people who lack this type of initiative is frustrating. As they sit around waiting for further instructions or permission to act, a countless number of growth opportunities pass them by. It's as if they are orchestrating the death of their career.

Business giant Conrad Hilton suggested, "Success seems to be connected with action. Successful people keep moving. They make mistakes, but they don't quit." People who take audacious action may not always be right but it's proof they are interested in doing more than staying busy—filling a hole. Besides, they normally keep on investing themselves until they get things right. They crush through old habits and move beyond the routine of doing the same things, the same way, every day.

We live in a fast-paced, impatient world that rewards the person who approaches each task with a sense of urgency. The world won't wait around for those who wait to be perfect before taking action. Focused energy, in the face of uncertainty, is rewarded.

Make yourself more valuable. Emphasize action. Don't get bogged down in purposeless activity. Seek radical achievement. There is always a hole to be filled. Don't wait for someone else to plant the tree. Take the initiative. Very little will be accomplished unless you go ahead and do it. Others will follow.

In the words of Theodore Roosevelt, "Get action. Do things; be sane, don't fritter away your time; create, act, take a place wherever you are and be somebody. Get action."

Four little words sum up what has lifted most successful individuals above the crowd: a little bit more. They did all that was expected of them and a little bit more.

A. LOU
VICKERY

SUCCESS IS
WHERE YOU
FIND IT

*Remember, when you can, that the definition of
success has changed. It is not only survival, the
having—it is the quality of every moment of
your life, the being. Success is not a
destination, a place you can ever get to;
it is the quality of the journey.*

JENNIFER JAMES

Success Is the Quality of the Journey

DEVELOP YOUR PICTURE
OF SUCCESS

The topic of success often produces two dominant questions: What is success? How do you attain it? My journey to answer these questions and understand success has taken a number of twists and turns. The older I get, the more reflective I become on the subject and the less dogmatic I am about my observations. I have concluded that people need to determine for themselves what success will mean to them.

A Thoroughbred horse never looks at the other horses. It just concentrates on running the fastest race it can.

HENRY FONDA

For me, that person is a success who enjoys life, lives it to the fullest, and helps others do the same. Success is ultimately an individual feeling of fulfillment, satisfaction, and a desire to continue growing. John Maxwell defined success in *The Success Journey* as "Knowing my purpose in life, growing to maximum potential, and sowing seeds that benefit others." In your lifelong success journey, Maxwell suggests, "Two things are required for success: the right picture of success and the right principles for getting there."

What is the right picture of success? Real-estate magnate Donald Trump suggested, "The real measure of success is how happy you are. I have a lot of friends who don't have a lot of money, but they are a lot happier than I am, so therefore I say that they are probably more successful." That's a nice thought, but there are countless people who are always searching for something more to make them happy. In fact, I'm convinced some people are only happy when they're unhappy. Happiness can certainly be one of many by-products of success, but rarely a measure of success.

Many other so-called success guideposts lead to equally miserable results. The attainment of the ideal job, achieving financial security, landing a major account, completing a challenging project, or building the dream home are empty measurements of success. That's not to say these aren't honorable pursuits, but when used as success indicators, they will fall far short of being classified as enduring factors.

I tend to concur with football great Joe Kapp who said, "Success is living up to your potential. That's all. Wake up with a smile and go after life. . . . Live it, enjoy it, taste it, smell it, feel it." Equally powerful is Ralph Waldo Emerson's reflection, "Laugh often; to win the respect of intelligent people and the affection of children; to appreciate honest criticism and endure the betrayal of false friends; to find the best in others; to leave the world a bit better; to know even one life has breathed easier because you have lived—this is to have succeeded." Successful people understand that success isn't some distant destination or a final achievement, but a process of successful living.

There's probably no one picture of success that suits everybody. Ultimately, it's up to you to decide and define what success means to you. Don't get caught up in what society, your co-workers, friends, or even extended family think is the definition of success. The difficulty of attempting to live up to others' expectations can be exasperating. Success is a highly personal thing and by deciding what the picture of success looks like, you set the stage to understand and pursue the principles that will get you there.

According to a 1993 *Pryor Report,* executives from 200 of the nation's largest companies were asked, "Of successful people you have met over the years, which of the following is the main reason for their success: (a) contacts, (b) determination, (c) hard work, (d) knowledge, or (e) luck?" In response, 40 percent of these high-powered executives indicated success was due to hard work and 38 percent said determination. Seventy-eight percent attributed success to hard work and determination.

A combination of hard work and determination define Olympic gold-medalist Janet Evans. She became the only American woman to win an Olympic individual swimming event. Evans, as a 17-year-old high school senior, took Seoul, Korea by storm in the fall of 1988. This Olympic wonder didn't settle for just one medal; she won three: the 400-meter freestyle, the 800-meter freestyle, and the 400-meter individual medley. If that isn't enough, Evans shattered her own world record with a 4:03.85 clocking in the 400-meter freestyle.

How was this young, untested Olympic swimmer able to excel under constant attention, pressure, and media focus? For five years prior, beginning at age 12, Evans committed herself to a rigorous daily training schedule. She began the day at 4:45 A.M. with a four-mile swim, followed by school, then homework, and back to the pool for a 9,000-meter swim. Janet was home by 6:00 for supper, a bit more homework, and in bed by 8:00 P.M. to prepare her body for another demanding day. Hard work and determination enabled Janet Evans to become the winner of 45 U.S. National Titles and the holder of six American records.

"But wait," you might say, "I thought success and achievement were not synonymous." When you combine knowing where you are going, striving to become your personal best, and helping others to do the same, with the qualities of hard work and unwavering dedication, good things happen. Janet Evans meshed together her picture of success and the required effort to attain it. "Success," suggests Brian Tracy, "comes from doing what you are ideally suited to do, doing it extremely well, and doing more and more of it."

Once you determine what your picture of success will look like, you might find the following suggestions helpful to clarify the principles that will guide your journey.

Basketball great Michael Jordan offered this insight: "Success isn't something you chase. It's something you have to put forth the effort for constantly. Then maybe it'll come when you least expect it. Most people don't understand that."

Author and professional speaker Carl Mays suggests, "The whole business of finding success is to make the most of who you are, with what you have, where you are."

"No one ever attains very eminent success by simply doing what is required of him," said Charles Kendall. "It is the amount and excellence of what is over and above the required that determines greatness."

When a reporter asked Thomas Edison to what he attributed his success, he replied, "The ability to apply my physical and mental energies to one problem incessantly without growing weary is my secret to success."

Violinist Isaac Stern believed, "There should be at least three cardinal rules for success in personal achievement, whatever the field may be: (1) complete passionate devotion to whatever field you have chosen; (2) the need to concentrate, to the exclusion of all else, when working on, thinking about, or executing whatever discipline you have chosen; (3) an utter pitiless sense of self-criticism, far greater than that which any outsider could give."

Booker T. Washington shared this interesting slant: "Success is not measured by the position one has reached in life, rather by the obstacles overcome while trying to succeed."

There's a wealth of practical advice in these success tidbits. You might even be able to add your own profound insight. One common theme permeates everything we read, hear, or experience about success—people who enjoy successful moments in their life are not couch potatoes waiting for success to happen. Successful people understand that success is all about who you are, and what you are doing every moment of your life to cause good things to happen.

Don't complicate the issue of success. Develop a clear picture of what success will mean to you and then endeavor to do something every day that will make that picture a reality.

WHAT IMPRESSION
WOULD YOU HAVE MADE?

You always do whatever you want to do. This is true of every act. Only you have the power to choose for yourself. The choice is yours. You hold the tiller. You can alter the course you choose in the direction of where you want to be—today, tomorrow, or in a distant time to come.

W. CLEMENT
STONE

❀

It's been quite a week. I've been flying in small commuter planes from one speaking engagement to another, sleeping in a variety of hotels, eating on the run, and attempting to be productive in airports. Although I immense-ly enjoyed every group I spoke to, I'm tired. Whenever I get tired, I get reflective.

Throughout the week I've strolled through airports observing uptight and stressed travelers. "What do you mean you can't deliver!" I overheard a sales person scream over the phone. "How could the flight leave without me?" demanded a frustrated vacationer. Countless people shuffled, ran, or slowly meandered through the airport hallways with a scowl on their face and pain in their eyes.

Two men, sitting near me on one flight, sounded like dueling banjos as they downgraded, bamblasted, and gener-ally ripped apart their companies. According to them, they weren't being paid enough, worked too many hours, and their bosses didn't have the slightest idea how difficult their jobs were. "Why in the world are they still on board?" I thought to myself.

Leonard, on the other hand, either loved his job at an airport coffee stand or he was preparing to audition for a professional acting career. His entertaining comments, happy feet, and friendly demeanor prompted me to increase the tip I had intended to give. I revisited him on my return through the airport later in the week. He was still there. Same song . . . second verse.

Bill loved his job as well. He told me so on our trip from the hotel to the airport. "Never thought I could enjoy work this much," this sixty-something courtesy van driver told me. He was genuinely interested in what I did for a living, had strong, positive feelings about his employer, and was well versed in the community and nation's current events. The 15-minute ride went far too fast. Bill gave courtesy drivers a *great* name.

Audrey also impressed me. She worked at the front desk of the Bismarck, North Dakota hotel where I was speaking. I had limited time after my seminar to get to the airport. I also needed to have the hotel send a box back to my office. Audrey immediately took charge, filled out the paperwork, weighed the box, smiled, and assured me she would personally take care of it. I extended my heartfelt thanks. "No problem," she responded, "that's what I'm here for." I like people like that!

Beau was equally impressive. He wore a seemingly permanently affixed massive smile across his face that only slightly diminished as he hoisted my heavy luggage into the van. "Is there somewhere we can stop on the way to the airport for a cup of gourmet coffee?" I asked. "You bet," he replied. He shared his passion for the theater and his aspirations to perform on stage. Beau had already experienced some acting success and was excited about his casting in an upcoming production of *Guys and Dolls.* I liked his spirit. He hadn't done anything special, except to make me feel good about my visit.

I'm on the final leg home. As we navigate the darkened skies, I'm watching a curly haired, blue-eyed two-and-a-half-year-old across the aisle and in front of me. This vibrant little thing hasn't yet realized it's night time. She sings. She laughs. She turns around to hold her daddy's hand as her big eyes look into his and she says, "I love you, Daddy!" Then she commences softly to sing her A-B-C's song. Through the crack in the seats, I can see her mother smile, nod approval, and struggle to stay awake.

Who will this little girl grow up to be? Will she become a rigid, uptight, stressed-out, weary adult? Or will she become another Leonardo, Audrey, Beau, or Bill? This sweet little thing has a multitude of choices to make as she grows up. These choices will determine who we see in 20, 30, or 40 years. I only hope she looks to those who have made responsible choices as her models.

Imagine that you are the adult that little girl models her life after. What will the result be? Will she love her chosen career? Will she find ways to positively affect the lives of people she comes in contact with? Will she continue smiling and innocently enjoying the little blessings of life? Will she face life's challenges with gusto and anticipation?

I endorse William Jennings Bryant's belief that "Destiny is not a matter of chance; but a matter of choice. It is not a thing to be waited for. It is a thing to be achieved." You can control your destiny and perspective of life, your job, and the people you encounter. The choices you make today, tomorrow, and next week build on each other to create a lifestyle that ultimately determines who you become, what you do, and what you have.

We can choose to welcome each new day with interest and curiosity, and as a new adventure, a new experience. We can also choose to dread every waking minute. We can choose to see an opportunity in every situation we encounter—or a crisis waiting to happen. We can choose to smile—or scowl. We can choose to plant seeds of fear, doubt, and dislike—or we can sow seeds of faith, hope, and love. We can choose to see others' positive characteristics and find them interesting and enjoyable—or we can choose to identify their annoyances and avoid interaction. The choice menu is endless.

I've learned you can give people a position or a job, but you cannot give them the qualities to be successful. People must choose whether or not to develop their qualities. Nothing will have a greater influence on your future than your decision to develop or bypass the characteristics of success.

Learning to love your job starts with understanding that you have choices. You are who you are and where you are today because of the choices you've made. If you want things to change, you have to make better choices. If you want to be a model of happiness, fulfillment, and contentment, eliminate the destructive choices that block these positive results. Act, walk, talk, and conduct yourself as the model person you can become. The only way you're going to make a change is to infuse yourself with a sense of urgency that continually nudges you to follow through.

Choose today to be the type of person that little girl on the airplane would be excited to become.

The common idea that success spoils people by making them vain, ego-tistical, and self-complacent is erroneous; on the contrary, it makes them, for the most part, humble, tolerant, and kind. Failure makes people bitter and cruel.

SOMERSET
MAUGHAM

THE MAKINGS
OF SUCCESS

*Success is
like Haley's
Comet, you
know. Every
now and then
it just comes
around.*

ROSS PEROT

*Dallas Times
Herald*

Success might just come around, but most often it is the result of focused and concentrated effort. Reflecting upon her years of public service, Margaret Thatcher suggested that "Success is having a flair for the things that you are doing. Knowing that is not enough, you have got to have hard work and a certain sense of purpose."

Tom Morris, in his book *True Success,* offers these guidelines for achieving success:

1. "A conception of what you want. This means a vision, goal or set of goals, 'powerfully imagined.'

2. "A confidence to see it through. Without it, you'll never overcome obstacles.

3. "A concentration on what it takes. Prepared and plan and do. 'The world has more participants, more catalysts, agents of change . . .'

4. "A consistency in what you do. Be stubborn and persistent—even after failure.

5. "A commitment of emotional energy. Emerson said, 'Nothing great was ever achieved without enthusiasm.'

6. "A character of high quality. Integrity inspires trust and gets people pulling for you.

7. "A capacity to enjoy the process. The journey should be fun as well as challenging."

I couldn't wait for success—so I went ahead without it.

JONATHAN WINTERS

As you can plainly see, there are no new-fangled success secrets. The principles, process, and disciplines of success have been around since the beginning of time. The real issue here is that we cannot enjoy the benefits of success without the investment of sacrifice. Those people who want to wake up successful need to wake up. It's not going to happen any other way. "Success, real success in any endeavor," says James Rouche, "demands more from an individual than most people are willing to offer—not more than they are capable of offering." In other words, none of the writings, principles, secrets, processes work . . . unless you do.

BREAK NEW GROUND

*I knew a man who grabbed a cat by the tail
and learned forty percent more about cats than
the man who didn't.*

MARK TWAIN

IT'S NOT
THAT BAD!

I can speak with experiential authority on the subject of mistakes. Although I'm not an advocate for making dumb mistakes on purpose, I've undoubtedly learned what to do and what not to do by doing what didn't work. If you're making any moves toward your goals or attempting to do things you've never done before, mistakes have probably become a normal part of your repertoire.

Mistakes are good for you. Motivational speaker Les Brown reminds us, "In order to get where you don't know you can go, you have to make mistakes to find out what you don't know." I know mistakes can be embarrassing, painful, and time consuming, but they are also marvelous teachers. In fact, going too long without a classic goof-up might be a serious indication that you've stopped learning, squelched your curiosity, or have settled into a comfort zone. It means you're aiming far too low and passing up the opportunity to pursue new levels of performance. That's dangerous. In fact, any one of these factors is the most serious mistake of all.

Every great mistake has a halfway moment, a split second when it can be recalled and perhaps remedied.

PEARL S. BUCK

Mistakes are learning tools, growing pains, and character builders you encounter on the way to your goals. They are friends most people would rather avoid. Who wants to be hanging around with an acquaintance named "foul-up"? But this friend will help you find out how good you really are. As Nelson Boswell observed, "The difference between greatness and mediocrity is often how an individual views mistakes."

To help you keep your mistakes in perspective, I've gleaned some classic mishaps from newspapers, the Internet, and articles that friends have forwarded to me. Maybe yours won't seem so bad. Hopefully, you can learn something from their performances. If nothing else, learn to have a sense of humor. Goldie Hawn says, "Once you can laugh at your own weaknesses, you can move forward. Comedy breaks down walls. It opens up people. If you're good, you can fill up those openings with something positive. Maybe you can combat some of the ugliness in the world."

New Women magazine declared Linda Evans the winner of the "Most Embarrassing Moment Contest." Here was her submission: "It was Christmas Eve, and I was on my feet all day working behind the cosmetics counter. I decided I should find a place to sit for a moment. I spied a tall plastic trash can and plopped down, resting my feet on a cardboard box. I allowed my body to ease into the can. About that time a few customers came to the register to check out, but I couldn't get out of the trash can. I was stuck; I couldn't believe it. The customers came around the counter to help me—some pulled my arms while others held the can. Then my manager came to the counter, wanting to know what was going on. He said he was going to call the fire department, who blasted in with sirens and lights. My hips had created a vacuum, so they had to cut me out of the trash can with a giant pair of scissors."

I guess you could say she got "canned" without being fired. I'm sure Linda would be the first one to admit that her mistake got her derriere in a jam.

How would you like to be Janice? She spent nearly her whole vacation sunbathing on the roof of her hotel. She wore a two-piece bathing suit the first few days, but always removed her glasses to ensure an even facial tan.

After several days she decided no one could see her way up there, so she slipped out of her suit to get a full body tan. She'd just gotten comfortable when she heard someone running up the outside stairs of the hotel. She was lying on her stomach, so she just pulled a towel over her bottom.

"Excuse me, miss," said the out-of-breath, sweating hotel manager. "The hotel doesn't mind you sunbathing on the roof, but we would appreciate you putting your suit back on."

"I'm sorry if I've violated some rule," Janice replied.

"It's not that," the manager calmly replied. "You're lying on the dining room skylight."

Oops!

The pastor of a small church prided himself on being sensitive to the needs of his parishioners. Moments before the Sunday morning service, he overheard a man complain about back pain. His wife quickly explained that Jack was recovering from surgery.

During the morning prayer, the pastor thought of Jack and prayed that he might recover from surgery and be "restored to full function." Chuckles scattered throughout the church.

Jack's surgery was a vasectomy. Even good intentions can turn into innocent mistakes.

Joe Lomusio recorded this embarrassing moment in his book *If I Should Die Before I Live*. A tourist was standing in line to buy an ice cream cone at a Thrifty Drug store in Beverly Hills. To her utter shock and amazement, who should walk in and stand right behind her but Paul Newman! Well, the lady, even though she was rattled, was determined to maintain her composure. She purchased her ice cream cone, turned confidently, and exited the store.

However, to her horror, she realized that she had left the counter without her ice cream cone! She waited a few minutes until she felt all was clear, and then went back into the store to claim her cone. As she approached the counter, the cone was not in the little circular receptacle, and for a moment she stood there pondering what might have happened to it. Then she felt a polite tap on her shoulder and, turning was confronted by—you guessed it—Paul Newman. The famous actor then told the lady that if she was looking for her ice cream cone, she had put it into her purse.

Copley High School was leading Wadsworth by only two points in a crucial basketball game. A Copley fan used a defensive strategy not in the playbook. Just as a Wadsworth player was about to throw an inbound pass, a 16-year-old Copley student pulled the player's shorts down to his knees. It was a classic example of "being caught with your pants down."

Wadsworth coach John Martin said, "It was a critical stage of the game, and it was a must-win for our team. Can you imagine what kind of concentration our kid had after he was exposed?"

We can only imagine! Of course, the student defensive player didn't fare so well either. After being charged with disrupting a lawful meeting and disorderly conduct, the boy was suspended from school for an unspecified number of days and banned from extracurricular activities.

Picture this one. A man decided to take advantage of his wife being away to paint the bathroom toilet seat. After he finished, he headed for the refrigerator to reward himself with a cold drink.

His wife came home sooner than expected and headed straight for the bathroom. She sat down and got the toilet seat stuck to her rear. Of course she got upset and panicked. She shouted to her husband to help. He immediately put an overcoat over her to cover the toilet seat and headed for the doctor.

Parading into the doctor's office, the husband lifted the coat to reveal the predicament. He looked at the doctor and asked, "Have you ever seen anything like this before?"

"Well, yes," the doctor replied. "But never framed."

The next time you're tempted to respond to your mistakes by organizing a self-pity party, reflect on the clumsy, ridiculous and self-deprecating boo-boo's experienced by others. Your slip-ups and bumbling acts might not seem so bad. At any rate, Charles Handy suggests, "It's not the mistake that hurts us, it's the grace we employ owning up to it that counts."

"Nobody makes mistakes on purpose," says Leo Burnett, founder of the advertising agency Leo Burnett, Inc. "When you do make a mistake, I urge that you shouldn't let it gnaw at you, but should get it out into the open quickly so it can be dealt with. And you'll sleep better, too."

MOVE THROUGH
YOUR FEARS

People are never
more insecure
than when they
become obsessed
with their fears
at the expense
of their dreams.

NORMAN
COUSINS

❊

According to a *Chicago Tribune* article entitled "Sign of the Times," police sharpshooters surrounded a car in Rochester, New York. In the back seat of the car was a man armed with a rifle. The police attempted to negotiate with the man but he refused to respond. The police patiently watched and waited until finally becoming suspicious. They made a surprising discovery: The armed man in the back seat was a mannequin.

When the owner of the car was found, he told the authorities he kept the mannequin in his car for protection. "You've got to do this," he said. "With the car-jackings, it helps if it looks like you've got a passenger."

We undoubtedly live in an age of fear. Horace Fletcher said, "Fear is an acid which is pumped into one's atmosphere. It causes mental, moral, and spiritual asphyxiation, and sometimes death; death to energy and all growth." Fear imprisons people. Fear keeps us from moving beyond where we are and from achieving our potential.

"Fear, to a degree," says Zig Ziglar, "makes procrastinators and cowards of us all." We all tend to possess mannequins intended to protect us from our fears.

Mannequins come in the form of low expectations, avoidance of risk, removal from potential conflict, shying away from new responsibilities, denying the reality of change or placing "do not touch" barriers around ourselves. These fear-protecting mannequins cause us to settle for far less than we are capable of and keep us from experiencing the fullness of life. As Edmund Burke said, "No passion so effectively robs the mind of all its powers of acting and reasoning as fear."

Swiss psychiatrist Paul Tournier, agreed: "All of us have reservoirs of our full potential, vast areas of great satisfaction, but the road that leads to those reservoirs is guarded by the dragon of fear."

This powerful life-stripping, adventure-robbing barrier is inside you. It's not the world . . . it's not your circumstances . . . it's not your job . . . it's not your past or the people in the present. It's the fear in you. The bad news is that fear sticks with us even when there is no real, concrete, or visible reason.

The good news is: Fear is learned and therefore can be unlearned. "Most fear is routed in ignorance," says Brian Tracy. "The more knowledge or skill you have in any area, the less fear it holds." It takes courage to overcome this fear-producing ignorance, but Karl A. Menninger reminded us that "Fears are educated into us and can, if we wish, be educated out."

The first and most difficult step in overcoming fear is courageous action. Professional boxing manager Cus D'Amato suggested, "The hero and the coward both feel exactly the same fear, only the hero confronts his fear and converts it to power." Everyone experiences fear one way or another. Only the victor makes an informed plunge forward.

In 1958 Woody Allen enjoyed a lucrative career as a comedy writer for television. He stayed behind the scenes because his biggest fear was appearing in front of an audience. Besides, the $75 a week stand-up comics were earning was only a token of the $1,700 he was earning doing the writing. Yet, Allen followed the urge to stretch beyond what he was doing. He got physically sick before every performance. He was applauded, booed, jeered, and cheered, but those who knew comedy revered him as a natural talent. "Talent is nothing," said Allen. "You're born with talent in the same way that basketball players are born tall. What really counts is courage. Do you have the courage to use the talent with which you were born?"

The great composer Ludwig van Beethoven lived much of his life fearing the possibility of deafness. How could anyone create a musical masterpiece without the benefit of hearing?

When that which he feared the most besieged him, Beethoven became frantic with anxiety. He consulted the specialists of his day and attempted every suggested remedy. Nothing worked.

Beethoven soon found himself living in a world of total quietness. He mustered the courage to move through his fear and the reality of deafness to write some of his finest musical masterpieces. The deafness shut out all distractions and the melodies flowed like never before. That which he had feared became a great asset.

Many people discover when coming face to face with their fear that their *fear* of fear was the only real fear. As Logan

Pearsall Smith put it, "What is more mortifying than to feel you have missed the plum for want of courage to shake the tree?" Fear possesses the powerful ability to hold us back, keep our talents in check, and cause us to miss life's fruit.

I would, in no way, want to give you the impression that fear can be mastered once and for all. Each time an event arises that surfaces your fear, you'll have to battle self-talk, imagination, expectations, and the memory of past experiences. Mentally work through the worst that could happen and the best possible thing that could happen if you were successful. Be realistic and, if at all possible, move forward. Fear is not overcome by merely thinking positive. By being realistic, a potentially overwhelming situation can be challenging, yet possible.

Action will reduce anxiety and tension, resulting in increased confidence and control.

"I believe that anyone can conquer fear," encouraged Eleanor Roosevelt, "by doing the things he fears to do, provided he keeps doing them until he gets a record of successful experiences behind him."

Realize that fear causes you to seek a comfort zone that holds you back from all that life has in store for you. Action propels you past these limitations toward the attainment of your goals and dreams. Move through your fears toward the realization of what you want and act as if it were impossible to fail.

What success really means is looking failure in the face and tossing the dice anyway. You may be the only person who ever knows how the dice come up, but in that know-ledge you have something that millions of people will never have— because they were afraid to try.

WRITER'S DIGEST

BE A TEAM PLAYER

People are playing different instruments with different parts, but when they perform together from the same musical score, they produce beautiful music. They produce value.

C. WILLIAM POLLARD
The Soul of the Firm

BECOME A
TRUST BUILDER

D o you trust the people you work with? Do they trust you? The answers to these two questions will reveal volumes about the quality of your work environment. J. W. Driscoll said, "Trust has been shown to be the most significant predictor of individuals' satisfaction with their organization."

Trust between co-workers isn't just a nicety; trust is a mandatory ingredient for relationships to grow. "Without trust, there can be no cooperation between people, teams, departments, divisions," wrote quality expert Edwards Deming. "Without trust, each component will protect its own immediate interests to its own long-term detriment, and to the detriment of the entire system." Consider that advice from a person who helped countless companies pursue their optimum performance. Deming's experience revealed the universal importance of trust to achieve quality, innovation, service, and productivity.

You can learn good manners to deal with people, but you can't learn to trust people. And you must trust to be comfortable with them.

PETER
DRUCKER

Low-trust environments struggle with rampant turnover, absenteeism, unresolved conflict, low morale, dissatisfied customers, and a direct negative affect on the bottom line. In low-trust environments, people tell you what you want to hear. There is apathy, backbiting, and disloyalty. Defensiveness, territorialism, and an unwillingness to take responsibility for mistakes are commonplace. People live in fear and suspicion. The ramifications are endless, inevitable, and costly.

Webster's defines trust as "assured reliance on the character, ability, strength or trust of someone or something." In other words, trust means to have faith in, or to believe in, someone or something. Although we are generally a trusting generation, we are at a profound stage in history. Distrust and skepticism are subtly replacing belief and talent.

Bill Kynes wrote in *A Hope That Will Not Disappoint:*

"We thought we could trust the military,
   but then came Vietnam;
"We thought we could trust the politicians,
   but then came Watergate;
"We thought we could trust the engineers,
   but then came the *Challenger* disaster;

"We thought we could trust our broker,
   but then came Black Monday;
"We thought we could trust the preachers,
   but then came PTL and Jimmy Swaggart.
"So who can I trust?"

You can no doubt add to the list reasons from recent events that discourage you from trusting.

"Trust is a calculated risk made with one's eyes open to the possibilities of failure," says Robert Levering, "but it is extended with the expectation of success."

This important organizational and relationship quality can be illustrated by the arrangement made between the shark and pilot fish. Sharks are renown for their indiscriminate palates and will enjoy a meal of almost any ocean dweller—that is, except the pilot fish. Instead, sharks extend an invitation for the pilot fish to join them for lunch; then, the smaller fish act as an automatic toothpick, eating the leftover food lodged between the sharks' teeth. It is a collaborative relationship; the shark gets clean teeth and better dental check-ups while the pilot fish gets nourished. Each fish is satisfied when the encounter is over.

Levering said trust is first of all a calculated risk. Second, it is extended with the expectation of success. So it is with the shark and pilot fish. First, the pilot fish trust the shark will not eat them and each fish knows that if it cooperates, their needs will be met.

I've hired hundreds of people in the past 25 years and have subscribed to one cardinal rule: Believe in and trust people until they prove themselves untrustworthy. In other words, trust begins with me, with my willingness to unconditionally trust other people. This goes against the common grain to wait for people to prove themselves before you trust them. Trust will breed trust. Mistrust breeds mistrust. The surest way to help people prove themselves trustworthy is to trust them.

In his little book *Illustrations of Bible Truth,* H.A. Ironside pointed out the foolishness of judging others. He related an incident in the life of a man called Bishop Potter. "He was sailing for Europe on one of the great transatlantic ocean liners. When he went on board, he found that another passenger was to share the cabin with him. After going to see the accommodations, he came up to the purser's desk and inquired if he could leave his gold watch and other valuables in the ship's safe. He explained that ordinarily he never availed himself of that privilege, but he had been to his cabin and had met the man who was to occupy the other berth. Judging from his appearance, he was afraid that he might not be a very trustworthy person. The purser accepted the responsibility for the valuables and remarked, 'It's all right, Bishop, I'll be very glad to take care of them for you. The other man has been up here and left his for the same reason.'" Trust is a risk game and the person who antes up first will ultimately be a winner.

You can help build an environment of trust with others. Incorporate the following seven principles in your daily activities.

1. Listen to people. Attempt to understand their feelings, perspectives, and experiences. Always keep sensitive and private information confidential. Seek out others' ideas. We trust people who make a sincere attempt to understand who we are and what we are about.

2. Be there for others. When we make time for people, recognize their effort, celebrate their accomplishments, and value their opinions, a trust bond develops. Look for the unique talents and abilities in those you work with and tell them what you see. Don't spend excessive time on your own agenda or focused on just your personal welfare.

3. Keep integrity intact. Demonstrate through your actions that people can unquestionably believe what you say, know you will keep your promises, and can be assured you will be open with them. In other words, walk the talk. Be sure your attitudes and actions are consistent with your words. This is probably the most powerful method for obtaining people's trust.

4. Refrain from gossip and feeding the grapevine. Untruths, exaggeration, and backbiting quickly suffocate trust. Get the facts. Deal with reality rather than hearsay. The truth isn't always easy to deal with, but healing the wounds caused by misinformation is always painful. Nurture a culture of straightforward, open, and honest communication.

5. Respect other people's values. Diversity is a fact of life. You can't ignore it. Although you may not agree or endorse someone else's lifestyle, learn to respect his or her position. When you know and appreciate what others believe, a candid relationship can be achieved. Close-minded people rarely build open relationships.

6. Care about people. This seems so simple, yet we tend to get so caught up in the busyness of doing and meeting demands that people's needs often take a back seat. The payoff for taking the time to really care about someone else's personal welfare is significant. Help others achieve their goals and maintain their self-esteem. Thoughtfulness, respect, kindness, and a belief in people will breed success and trust.

7. Mend broken fences. Be willing to admit mistakes. Ask forgiveness. Restore peace where conflict has caused tension. Unhealed wounds will fester and infect relationships. Resist pointing an accusing finger when things go wrong. Take personal responsibility. Make amends.

Like all other relationship components, there is no magic formula for making trust suddenly appear. Trust isn't something we give attention to from nine to five; it requires a way of life that consistently displays, at minimum, the seven core principles for building trust. It takes an incredible commitment to develop the persistence, the patience, and the discipline to hold a relationship together for the long haul. Trust lies at the heart of this endeavor and consistency is the path that leads you there.

The best proof of love is trust.
JOYCE BROTHERS

WE ARE
THE TEAM

*The most
important
measure of
how good a
game I played
was how much
better I'd made
my teammates
play.*

Bill Russell

❋

One of the often overlooked benefits and responsibilities of teamwork is how we make others look.
Dynamic teams are composed of people who tend
to possess a genuine desire to make the team look good by
their performance. When team members fail to grasp this
concept and not live up to their end of the deal, it reflects on
the image of the entire team. Let me show you what I mean.

A 3-1/2 hour layover at Chicago O'Hare on a sunny and
warm April Sunday afternoon is not on my top ten list of
"Most Desirable Things to Do!" Unboarding the plane, my
mind raced through ideas that would help me endure this
boring necessity. Being a people-watcher holds my attention
for a short time and then I'm looking for other avenues to
pass time.

Bookstores always draw my attention and often tap my
wallet. I found one a short distance from my departure gate
and decided to invest some time browsing the latest titles,

reading a few pages here and there, and generally "sampling" the merchandise. Convinced an hour had passed, I reentered the corridor and glanced at my watch. It stopped running. No wait, the second hand was moving. Only 12 minutes had elapsed. Now what?

The smell of freshly brewed gourmet coffee is a second temptation to which I often succumb. Ordering the biggest cup they offered and purchasing an equally tempting pastry, I decided to make my way to the seating area at the gate and wait out my layover.

As I entered the end of the terminal on "B" concourse, my eyes fell on a young man sitting in a wheelchair with a heavy coat on, zipped up to his neck. His head was cocked back, eyes were tightly closed, and it was evident he was soundly sleeping.

"How sad," I thought to myself. "Here is a young man who could be making something of himself. Instead, he's homeless and comes to the airport to sleep off his nightly activities."

I continued reading a book I started earlier on the trip, and periodically glanced over at the limp body that hadn't moved since I sat down.

THE SIMPLE SECRETS of HAPPINESS

"What could he be dreaming about? Where will he go when he finally awakens? What awaits him in his day-to-day surroundings?"

"Hey, Jimmy!" a powerful voice blared behind me.

The young man was startled awake.

"You on break?"

"No," he responded groggily. "Can't you see I'm working?"

"Then I need you to push this lady to gate B-2. She has a plane to catch in 15 minutes."

"Ah, man," he responded as he slowly removed his heavy coat and threw it over the bench next to him.

To my surprise, he was dressed in the uniform of the airlines I was flying with. I had to smile. Here I was judging and stereotyping without having the facts. The sad thing is, the facts were as bad as my misguided conclusions. What I had just witnessed had to be a fluke.

To say he was excited about performing his duties would be a drastic overstatement. His eyes were open but his mind hadn't told his feet to start functioning. He shuffled behind the wheelchair, slowly pushing his elderly customer to her destination.

I stayed glued to my seat to observe how this situation would unfold. Would the lady in her wheelchair make her flight? Would Jimmy return to resume his nap? How would the airline employees respond?

Upon Jimmy's return to the area (which took place as slowly as he had exited), a few cohorts arrived to visit. "Gee, I hate it when the old bag wakes me up," he told his friends. "I was really enjoying myself. What time is it anyway?" When the conversation with his buddies ended, he put his coat back on, zipped it up, and resumed his sleeping position.

I couldn't believe my ears. This was no homeless, destitute, unwanted person. He was an airline employee bothered by the command to wake up and do his job. When I left the area an hour later, his mouth was hanging wide open as he periodically engaged in a gross sounding cough/snore. Not one employee questioned his status as they paraded by. He lived and worked (I use the term loosely) in his own world.

I spent that flight reflecting on how Jimmy's behavior clouded my perceptions of the entire airline. Not one of Jimmy's teammates said anything to him about his lethargic, unprofessional, lazy behavior. I wondered if they realized the

*The main
ingredient
of stardom
is the rest of
the team.*

John Wooden

❋

impression he gave to the rest of the airline employees. Did they really want to be associated with such incompetence?

The more I thought, the more infuriated I became. But wait a minute. How many times are we guilty of excusing the performance of people on our teams with such justification as "That's just the way Jimmy is." "Mary has always been negative." "Pete just isn't a team player." "Sally has never had much get up and go."

Coach John Wooden believed that if everyone does not accept his or her role and play it to the best of his or her ability, "the group as a whole is going to suffer." Through our consistent, active participation, we can help our team develop a winning reputation.

PRACTICE THE
ART OF ENCOURAGEMENT

asketball great Michael Jordan was asked by columnist Bob Greene why he wanted his father to be in the stands during a basketball game. Jordan replied, "When he's there, I know I have at least one fan." No matter how strong, self-confident, popular, or competent you are, feeling the support of a loyal fan can be just the encouragement you need to make it through a new challenge, difficult project, or even a tedious task.

Likewise, you can be that loyal fan for other people. Oftentimes people become so concerned about not being able to do great things for someone else that they neglect to do the little things that can be equally as meaningful and effective. One of those "little things" you can do is to provide encouragement. Somebody once said, "Encouragement is the fuel for tomorrow." Encouragement rewards people for who they are and gives them hope in doing all they can do and becoming all they can be.

Flatter me, and I may not believe you. Criticize me, and I may like you. Ignore me, and I may not forgive you. Encourage me, and I will not forget you.
WILLIAM ARTHUR WARD

Many years ago, an interesting experiment was conducted to measure people's ability to endure pain. Psychologists were interested in measuring how long a barefoot person could stand in a bucket of ice water. (Anyone who has ever had a severely sprained ankle understands the discomfort in this exercise.) Anyway, experiment results showed that one factor significantly affected some people's ability to endure the pain twice as long as others. The common factor was encouragement. Those people who had someone nearby giving support and encouragement were able to endure the pain much longer than those who were left to themselves.

We all know how the smallest gesture, kind comment, genuine word of encouragement, quick compliment, or praise for a job well done can make a lasting difference in someone's life. Yet, we don't always take the time to let people know our heartfelt thoughts and give them a small gift of happiness.

Find a 3 x 5 note card. Think about one person you work with who could benefit from a personal message that would make him or her feel good about him- or herself. Choose whatever quality, talent, action that you have observed in that person's life. What is it about that person that you appreciate? Why are you glad to have the privilege of working with this person? What has this person done this week to make you smile, lift a load, or add value to the team?

Make your message personal. Use the person's first name. Write your message of encouragement in the first person and express how you feel about the person. Be as specific as you can. Orison Swett Marden believed, "There is no investment you can make which will pay you so well as the effort to scatter sunshine and good cheer through your establishment." That's exactly what this little exercise is intended to do.

Help people believe in themselves. Build their confidence and self-esteem. Make a concentrated effort to see that people feel important and appreciated. Celebrate and get excited about others' successes. Be a cheerleader. Point out strengths and contributions. Bring a ray of sunshine with you to work everyday and scatter it liberally wherever you go.

You can be a hero in your organization by becoming a picker-upper person. Make it a way of life rather than a periodic or one-time event.

We all need encouragement. We can live without it just as a young tree can live without fertilizer, but unless we receive that warm nurturing, we never reach our full potential, and like the tree left to itself, we seldom bear fruit.
FLORENCE
LITTAUER

LOOSEN UP...
LIGHTEN UP...
HAVE FUN!

*A fun working environment is much more
productive than a routine environment.
People who enjoy their work will come up with
more ideas. The fun is contagious.*

ROGER VON OECH

AN ENTERTAINING
FLIGHT ATTENDANT

G ood morning, ladies and gentlemen! Welcome aboard United Airlines flight 548, direct from Palm Springs to Chicago."

Wait a minute! My mind starts racing. I know it's early in the morning, 6:50 A.M. to be exact, but I was sure this flight went to Denver.

"Now that I got your attention," the voice continues, "my name is Annamarie and I'll be your first flight attendant today. Actually, we will be en route to Denver so if you were not planning to go there, now would be a good time to get off the plane.

"Safety is important to us so please take out the safety card in the pocket in front of you and acquaint yourself with the procedures. Come on, everybody, take out those brochures and wave them in the air! (70% of the passengers chuckle and do as they are told; 20% aren't awake yet; and the other 10% are sourpusses) Thank you. Thank you.

I have always been able to gain my living without doing any work. I enjoyed the writing of books and magazine matter; it was merely billiards to me.

MARK TWAIN

"In the event that we mistakenly land in a body of water, a decision must be made. You can either pray and swim like crazy, or use your seat as a flotation device.

"We will be serving breakfast in flight this morning. On the menu I have eggs benedict and fruit crepes . . . not really, but they sound good to me. However, the flight attendants will be offering your choice of an omelet or cold cereal."

William Faulkner once lamented that "The saddest thing in life is that the only thing we can do for eight hours a day, day after day, is work. We can't eat for eight hours a day, or drink for eight hours a day, or make love for eight hours a day. All that we can do for that long a period," he said, "is work, which is the reason man makes himself and everybody so miserable and unhappy."

I'm thankful the flight attendant on flight 548 didn't possess Faulkner's attitude about work. It was evident she enjoyed what she did. Her entertaining approach to a normally routine, boring takeoff procedure endeared her to the passengers. Think of the innumerable benefits people would experience were they to add this positive approach to their normal routine.

John Maxwell summed it up quite well when he said, "I choose to have fun. Fun creates enjoyment. Enjoyment invites participation. Participation focuses attention. Attention expands awareness. Awareness promotes insight. Insight generates knowledge. Knowledge facilitates action. Action yields results."

PUT YOUR WORK
IN PERSPECTIVE

*The master in
the art of living
makes little
distinction
between his
work and his
play, his labor
and his
leisure . . .
He hardly
knows which is
which.*

JAMES A.
MICHENER

✿

I'm almost embarrassed to admit it, but about once a year I find myself rewatching and enjoying The *Mighty Ducks,* the highly successful Disney movie about a youth hockey team that rises from anonymity to celebrity.

The movie opens with a flashback scene of a demanding, tough, overbearing hockey coach convincing a young player, Gordon Bombay, to attempt a crucial penalty shot. "If you miss this shot," he says, "you'll let me down and you'll let your team down!" The frightened boy manipulates the puck, takes his best shot, and barely misses the goal. The burden of that loss and the shame of letting his team down dramatically affects Gordon Bombay for years to come.

Bombay unexpectedly becomes the coach of a group of struggling youth called the District Five Ducks. They know they are bad and Bombay reinforces all the bad they believe about themselves. He berates them, insults them, teaches them to cheat, and continually pressures them to meet unrealistic expectations. He becomes the coach he had as a youth . . . and hates it.

Gordon Bombay gradually learns that having fun on the ice is a worthy goal of any player or coach. The *Mighty Ducks* learn to believe in themselves, support each other, refine their skills, and have fun playing hockey. Bombay works hard to nurture the enjoyment of the game in his young skaters, and in the closing chapter of the movie, he takes his team of Ducks into a championship playoff game. The opposing top-rated team is tough, big, mean, and coached by none other than his old coach, Jack Riley.

Riley's strategy hasn't changed a bit. He berates. He insults. He threatens. Bombay has endorsed a different approach. "More fun! More fun!" the team chants in the huddle with Bombay leading the cheer.

The Hawks and the Ducks skate to a 4–4 tie as the final gun sounds. But one of the Hawks has fouled a Duck player, giving the Ducks a penalty shot—one chance to win the championship.

Coach Bombay chooses Charlie Conway to take the final shot. Bombay's touching dialog with Charlie is the exact opposite of the conversation in the opening scene of the movie. "You may make it, you may not," Coach Bombay tells Charlie. "But that doesn't matter. What matters is that we're here. Look around. Who'd ever have thought we would make it this far? Take your best shot. I believe in you, Charlie, win or lose."

Charlie grins, accepts the challenge, and sends the puck into the opponent's goal. The underdog Ducks win the championship.

I like this movie a lot because it portrays the type of environment and message needed in our organizations and personal careers. Willie Stargell, the retired baseball star, once remarked that at the start of a ballgame, you never hear an umpire yelling "Work ball." Of course not. They always yell "Play ball!" Let me push this a bit further. I wonder what would happen if the people you work with started every work day reminding themselves "I get to play today." Work should be a fun, marvelous, exciting game.

Instead, I run into people in a variety of careers who struggle with:

- Low self-esteem
- Feeling overwhelmed by job and people demands
- Uncertainty about their future

- Feelings of powerlessness to make things better
- Busyness without results
- A lack of meaning and satisfaction in their work
- Routine, monotony, and boredom

People say they don't have time to have fun anymore, or they can't wait until the weekend so they can live again. Other people view their work as an interruption between free hours. Pressure, stress, and loss of control haunt still others. Edward L. Bernays reminds us, "Never permit a dichotomy to rule your life, a dichotomy in which you hate what you do so you can have pleasure in your spare time. Look for a situation in which your work will give you as much happiness as your spare time." What marvelous advice!

The *Mighty Ducks* movie tends to put things in perspective. Work is meant to be enjoyed. In fact, when you learn to relax, enjoy the hours, refine your skills, give your best, and nurture those around you, a refreshing attitude of satisfaction will evolve. Try it. See for yourself that the pressure cooker many of us work in can be relieved by the soothing efforts of others, and by taking responsibility for self-induced negative feelings and thoughts about what we do for a living.

Love what you're doing and don't retire... I would rather be a failure at something I love than a success at something I hate.

George Burns

"Work is a four-letter word," suggested Al Sacharov. "It's up to us to decide whether that four-letter word reads 'drag' or 'love.' Most work is a drag because it doesn't nourish our souls. The key is to trust your heart to move where your talents can flourish. This old world will really spin when work becomes a joyous expression of the soul."

REFILLS ARE
FREE

The short 36 minute flight wasn't enough time for the flight attendants to serve beverages. Considering the early morning hour, most of us quickly made our way to the nearest airport coffee shop as soon as we exited the plane.

I took my place in line behind the other 20 caffeine-deprived travelers. We were all entertained watching and listening to the server behind the counter. She was singing along with the oldies music on the radio, dancing, taking orders, working the cash register, flipping cups (before filling), and serving the coffee and goodies. If she didn't thoroughly enjoy her job, someone should nominate her for an Emmy award-winning performance.

As I approached the counter to place my order, she continued to entertain the customers with her perky personality. The man behind me jokingly commented, "You've got to get over this depression."

We can determine our optimum speed of living by trying various speeds and finding out which one is most agreeable.

HANS SELYE

Misunderstanding his attempt at humor and unable to clearly hear what he said, she quickly replied, "Pressure? What pressure? I don't feel any pressure!"

I seemed to enjoy that morning's coffee a bit more than usual as I reflected on the events that had just taken place at the coffee bar. Here was a barista who had clearly decided her optimum speed of living. Because she was energetic, gregarious, fun-loving, and friendly at 7:00 A.M., some people were suspicious of her behavior. How could anyone move at that pace this early and enjoy what she was doing?

I'm finding it increasingly curious how moving slow, being sarcastic and negative, disliking your job, and dragging your way through life is considered normal. But show a little positive emotion, smile, and enjoy the day, and you're a candidate for being labeled unrealistic.

The truth is, we each choose our optimum speed and nature of living. Unfortunately, some people have quit trying anything but the rut to which they are accustomed. That's their choice. It's unfortunate, but until they decide to put a little zip in their step, they'll continue to reap mediocre results.

I like being with people who like life. I enjoy the company of friends who enjoy their work. I choose to spend time with people who choose to make the most of every moment they're breathing. Hang around these kinds of people and they will help you continually adjust and improve your speed of living.

I think I'll go back for a refill. I could use a little inspiration.

One of the symptoms of an approaching nervous break-down is the belief that one's work is terribly important.

BERTRAND
RUSSELL

HAVE A LITTLE
FUN

He who does
not get fun
and enjoyment
out of every
day . . . needs
to reorganize
his life.

George
Matthew
Adams

❈

A few years ago, my wife gave me a gift certificate on Valentine's Day for a one-hour massage. I've never indulged the services of a massage therapist but it sounded like a fun experience so I immediately called for an appointment.

Let me preface the remainder of this story with a bit of insight about my personality. I enjoy a periodic practical joke that creates a bit of humor or good clean fun. I normally reserve such antics for people I know well, but this day, a rare opportunity surfaced I just couldn't resist.

The therapist greeted me in her lobby and, after a bit of small talk, she asked what type of massage I preferred. I weighed the options and decided on deep muscle therapy. The therapist was cordial and professional as she led me into the room and turned on some "mood" music, assembled her lotions and lit a few scented candles. Then it happened.

"Glenn, I'm going to leave the room for a few minutes," she said. "Would you please disrobe down to your underwear."

I mustered a serious expression and replied, "I don't wear underwear!"

The laughter that followed, once she realized I was only kidding, probably stimulated more endorphins than the massage that followed.

I feel sorry for people whose lives are so regimented that they are unable to produce, or at least enjoy, periodic doses of fun. I realize fun isn't for everyone. It's only for people who want to enjoy life and feel alive. For all others, there is tension, stress, ulcers, headaches, and boredom. The decision on which path to take sounds like a no-brainer to me.

Charlie Chaplin said, "If you've got something funny to do, you don't have to be funny to do it." You don't have to change your personality to have fun. It does require you to look for the ridiculous, slightly humorous, absurd, entertaining events in everyday life. Having fun isn't something you necessarily learn; it is a perspective on life that you give yourself permission to enjoy.

*A light heart
lives long.*

*William
Shakespeare*

❊

As I drove through a small town in southern Iowa, I noticed a fun-loving radiator repair shop that posted this motto on its sign: "The best place in town to take a leak." I was equally impressed with some plumbers who approached their business with a bit of levity. Painted across the side of their van was this saying: "In our business, a fush beats a full house." That's the kind of plumber I want doing my work. Finally, a muffler shop in a small town in Nebraska made this attempt at fun: "No appointment necessary. We'll hear you coming." The people responsible for these signs have given themselves permission to express a perspective on life that produces a little fun.

Consider again the words of George Matthew Adams: "He who does not get fun and enjoyment out of every day . . . needs to reorganize his life." Is it time for you to do a little reorganizing?

Glen Van Ekeren is Executive Vice President of Vetter Health Services. Previously he served as Director of People Development for Village Northwest Unlimited, an organization dedicated to meeting the needs of people with disabilities, and as President of People Building Institute, a seminar and consulting company committed to maximizing people and organizational potential. He shares his relationship principles with diverse audiences across the country as a frequent speaker and keynote presenter. He is the author of the *Speaker's Sourcebook* and *The Speaker's Sourcebook II*, and a featured author in several *Chicken Soup for the Soul* books.

Roberta Wilson
5-22-02